Melanie Smicek

American Dreams, Suburban Nightmares

Suburbia as a Narrative Space between Utopia
and Dystopia in Contemporary American Cinema

Anchor Academic
Publishing

Smicek, Melanie: American Dreams, Suburban Nightmares: Suburbia as a Narrative Space between Utopia and Dystopia in Contemporary American Cinema, Hamburg, Anchor Academic Publishing 2014

Buch-ISBN: 978-3-95489-321-8
PDF-eBook-ISBN: 978-3-95489-821-3
Druck/Herstellung: Anchor Academic Publishing, Hamburg, 2014

Bibliografische Information der Deutschen Nationalbibliothek:
Die Deutsche Nationalbibliothek verzeichnet diese Publikation in der Deutschen Nationalbibliografie; detaillierte bibliografische Daten sind im Internet über http://dnb.d-nb.de abrufbar.

Bibliographical Information of the German National Library:
The German National Library lists this publication in the German National Bibliography. Detailed bibliographic data can be found at: http://dnb.d-nb.de

© Anchor Academic Publishing, Imprint der Diplomica Verlag GmbH
Hermannstal 119k, 22119 Hamburg
http://www.diplomica-verlag.de, Hamburg 2014
Printed in Germany

Contents

1 Introduction 1

2 Suburbia as physical and cultural space in the USA 4

2.1 The history of the suburbanization of the USA 4

2.2 The concept of suburbia as a cultural space 7

3 Utopian and dystopian narratives of suburbia 11

4 Suburbia in contemporary American cinema 14

4.1 Film as narrative space 14

4.2 The invention of reality: Simulations, simulacra, suburbia 15

4.3 Suburbia as setting and center of contemporary American Films:
   Introduction to the film analyses 16

5 Once upon a time: Suburbia as nostalgic utopia in *Pleasantville* 18

5.1 Introduction and plot summary 18

5.2 The opening scenes: Real vs. nostalgic visions of suburbia 19

5.3 The utopia of *Pleasantville* 21

5.4 Exploring utopia: The suburban space of Pleasantville 22

5.5 The creation of new spaces in Pleasantville 24

5.6 The end of paradise: Fall of Man, racism and visions of dystopia 26

5.7 Happy ever after? A summarizing reading of *Pleasantville* 29

6 Better than reality? Suburbia as simulacra in *The Truman Show* 31

6.1 Introduction and plot summary 31

6.2 Different layers of diegesis: Utopian and dystopian perspectives in
   The Truman Show 32

6.3 The space of Seahaven: The utopian artifice of suburbia 34

6.4 Seahaven between simulacra and simulation 36

6.5 "On the air. Unaware": Surveillance and control in *The Truman Show* ... 39

6.6 Truman's escape from dystopia: hope for suburbia? 41

7 "Look Closer": Suburbia as imprisoning dystopia in *American Beauty* 43

7.1 Introduction and plot summary.. 43

7.2 Utopia or dystopia? The introduction of the suburban space of
   American Beauty.. 43

7.3 Defining the dystopia of *American Beauty*: Suburbia as a prison.............. 46

7.4 The destructiveness of the American Dream in suburbia.......................... 48

7.5 The suburbs as "picture windows": Voyeurism and control in suburbia ... 49

7.6 Hope for suburbia? The search for the true beauty in dystopia................. 51

8 Conclusion and outlook 54

List of figures.. 56

Works Cited.. 60

1. Introduction

> [Suburbia] has become the quintessential physical achievement of the United States; it is perhaps more representative of its culture than big cars, tall buildings, or professional football. Suburbia symbolizes the fullest, most unadulterated embodiment of contemporary culture.[1]

As Kenneth Jackson notes in his price-winning chronicle *Crabgrass Frontier*, the suburban landscape has become inseparable from American culture within the last two centuries. Nowadays living in the suburbs is the norm for most Americans, as since the 1990s, more than two third of the population lives in suburban districts. The term *suburbia* does not only relate to the geographical concept that differentiates these dwellings from urban or rural areas, but also describes a cultural, ideological space incorporating Americans' hopes for an economically safe and prosperous family life. Closely tied to the history and culture of the USA, suburbia marks a dynamic ideological space that is constantly influenced and recreated by both the events of everyday life and artistic discourse. Thus, the depiction of suburban life functions as a central narrative element in numerous works of American literature, art and film. In this context, fictional texts do not merely *represent* suburbia, but also have a decisive role in the *shaping* of suburban spaces.

The treatment of suburbia as a cultural space in American movies is of special interest, as their commercial success and popularity make films important cultural texts.[2] As Spigel notes, "television and new media redirect our experience of private and public spheres"[3] and therefore highly influence our perceptions of the spaces we inhabit. Regarding suburban landscapes, this aspect is particularly interesting because the inexorable rise of the television practically coincided with the postwar suburbanization of the US and had a significant effect on life in general and on the suburban ideal in particular. As a consequence, the TV-set was inseparable from the model of the suburban single-home in the 1950s. Thus, already in the fifties, when the idealized image of suburbia evolved, television had a decisive impact on the creation of suburbia as a cultural space. In this context, it must be questioned whether the depictions of suburbia are simulations of the real spaces, or if it is in fact the other way around, so that suburbia as a cultural concept is a mere simulation of the fictional spaces depicted on screen and thus a copy without an original[4].

---

[1] Jackson, Kenneth. *Crabgrass Frontier: The Suburbanization of the United States.* New York: Oxford University Press 1985, p. 4

[2] Cf. Halper, Thomas; Muzzio, Douglas. "Pleasantville? The Suburb and its Representation in American Movies". In: *Urban Affairs Review*, 37 (March 2002), pp. 544-545

[3] Spigel, Lynn. *Welcome to the Dreamhouse: Popular Media and Postwar Suburbs.* Durham: Duke University Press 2001, p. 10

[4] Jean Baudrillard's definition of the simulacrum will support the discussion in Chapter 4.

Before analyzing fictional representations of suburbia, it is necessary to first look at the historical development of the suburbs and to explore how the cultural space of suburbia has been formed in the course of history. As I will discuss in the following chapter, the rapid suburbanization of the USA was mostly triggered in the aftermath of the Second World War, when suburbia promised the returning soldiers and their young families a peaceful life in homogeneous and green communities outside of the ever growing metropolises. For the veterans who were financially supported by the government, the suburbs proposed an opportunity to raise their children in decent, quiet and safe environments while nevertheless being able to have their jobs in the big cities. As a consequence, homeownership and suburban dwelling became closely linked to the American Dream in the postwar period.

More than fifty years after the war, the contemporary suburbia deviates from the concept of the suburbs projected in the 1950s, particularly due to high divorce rates and the increase of crime facing not only urbanites but also the residents of suburban areas. Nevertheless, the nostalgic view of the suburbs as the "Promised Land", an image closely tied to the postwar era, has survived in the minds of many Americans until today. As Hayden puts it, suburbia is still the "landscape of the imagination where Americans situate ambitions for upward mobility and economic security, ideals about freedom and private property, and longings for social harmony and spiritual uplift"[5]. Postwar critics have long objected this view, considering the suburbs rather as overly controlled, depressing landscapes of mass-consumption, conformity and alienation. The reasons for this criticism are to be found in the "vision of the suburbs defined by endless malls, tidy streets with manufactured lawns, and houses with little character"[6] and therefore in the uniformity of suburban landscape design in general. Hence, today the suburbs are mostly regarded as "either *utopian* models of community or *dystopian* landscapes of dispiriting homogeneity" and therefore "remain a contested, if only superficially understood, terrain"[7]. The explanation of the utopia/dystopia dichotomy in terms of the representation of suburbia in fictional works is the focus of interest in the third chapter of this book.

After an evaluation of films as narrative spaces in general and their potential to shape the spectators' perceptions of spaces in the fourth chapter, I will exemplify the dualistic representation of suburbs in contemporary American cinema by analyzing Gary Ross's *Pleasantville* (1998), Peter Weir's *The Truman Show* (1998) and Sam Mendes's *American*

---

[5] Hayden, Dolores. *Building Suburbia. Green Fields and Urban Growth, 1820-2000.* New York: Pantheon Books 2003, p. 3
[6] Baxandall, Rosalyn; Ewen, Elizabeth. *Picture Windows: How the Suburbs Happened.* New York: Basic Books 2000, p. xv
[7] Beuka, Robert. *SuburbiaNation: Reading Suburban Landscape in Twentieth-Century American Fiction and Film.* New York: Palgrave Macmillan 2004, p. 7; emphasis added.

Beauty (1999). As postmodern texts, these films critically examine the tension between utopian and dystopian perspectives on suburbia and question the validity of the mystification of the suburb as a space incorporating the American Dream. All three of them can be categorized as satirical (comedy-) dramas focusing, generally speaking, on their male protagonists' search for the sense of life in a dysfunctional suburban landscape. By studying these films in terms of narrative techniques, cinematic realization and the portrayal of the suburban spaces presented on screen, I will explore the depicted divergence between the nostalgic, utopian ideal of suburbia and the dystopian concept connected to the problems of contemporary suburban living, like the collapse of the nuclear family, the breakdown of moral values, and particularly the occupation of private life by modern technology. By relating these fictional works to both the historical development of the suburbs and the significance of suburbia as a cultural artifact of the USA, I will examine how utopian concepts of suburbia are created both culturally and psychologically in the films, and how the underlying anxieties of the suburban experience, visualized by the employed dystopian narratives, challenge this ideal.

2. Suburbia as physical and cultural space in the USA

2.1 The history of the suburbanization of the USA

The origins of the suburban structure found in the USA today can be traced back to the first half of the nineteenth century, when "America's largest cities underwent a dramatic spatial change"[8]. New transportation devices such as the steam ferry, omnibuses and the commuter railroad resulted in a first wave of mass immigration which literally transformed urban landscapes, leading to substantial rethinking and the urge to separate "work and residence in American cities".[9] The emergence of the first suburban homes was developed by a number of well known publicists in the mid-nineteenth century, particularly by Frederick Law Olmsted who inter alia designed Central Park in Manhattan, the educator Catherine Beecher and the landscape architect Andrew Jackson Downing. Olmsted drew his inspiration for his later landscaping and suburban planning projects from his trip to Birkenhead Park near Liverpool, a park area that "was surrounded [...] by a picturesque suburb"[10]. He claimed that "leisure and metropolis were mutually exclusive"[11] and that conscious and careful planning of suburban neighborhoods was necessary to ensure decent dwelling for residents. At the same time, the first typical American suburban houses were designed by Beecher and Downing, being "promoted by small builders and the editors of women's magazines"[12]. Beecher's *Treatise on Domestic Economy*, published in 1841, served as "the first American book to offer plans for the practical dwelling"[13] and became the central work to portray American domestic philosophy.

The first true suburban boom took place in the 1920s, when the automotive revolution and the expansion of electricity gave "working and middle-class people the opportunity to move from congested cities to spacious suburbs"[14]. From this time onwards, the car functioned as "the connective tissue between home, work and [...] consumption"[15] and therefore marked a central element of the suburban development. Alongside the automotive revolution, there was also a profound change in the real-estate sector, as housing in the outer areas accessible only by car became much cheaper than in the cities. The rise of the advertising industry also played

---

[8] Jackson 1985, p. 20

[9] Fishman, Robert. *Bourgeois Utopias: The Rise and Fall of Suburbia*. New York: Basic Books 1987, p. 116

[10] Ibid., p. 104

[11] Kenyon, Amy Maria. *Dreaming Suburbia: Detroit and the Production of Postwar Space and Culture*. Detroit: Wayne State University Press 2004, p. 149

[12] Hayden, Dolores. *Redesigning the American Dream: The Future of Housing, Work, and Family Life*. New York: Norton 2002, p. 38

[13] Jackson 1985, p. 62

[14] Baxandall and Ewen 2000, p. 41

[15] Ibid., p. 48

an important role in the expansion process of suburban areas, as "advertisers promoted the private suburban dwelling as a setting for other purchases"[16], depicting the single house as the true center of a happy family life. As a response to the technological changes, a group of intellectuals, among them urban planners, social critics and architects, formed the Regional Plan Association of America (RPAA), a collective that focused on new models of community planning and organization. Their central vision was to build communities "with well-made, efficient, affordable houses and space for both pedestrians and cars"[17], mixing parks and leisure areas with modern road systems, which would make it possible for residents to combine their private and working lives effectively. The group performed innovative experiments in planned housing particularly in the outer areas of New York, for instance by designing the suburban communities of Sunnyside Gardens in Queens and Radburn, New Jersey. Although these projects could not solve the problem of "one third of a nation remain[ing] ill-housed in tenements and slums"[18], their ideas were visionary as they shaped public views of community planning and dwelling and also had a great influence on the New Deal programs of the Roosevelt Administration to follow.

When the Great Depression took place in the 1930s, many Americans suffered from mass-unemployment, poverty and homelessness in a way they had never experienced before. As a reaction to the desperate financial situation, the government around President Roosevelt installed the so called New Deal, a series of strategies that aimed at helping the USA to recover economically. With regard to the housing sector, the two schemes that had the most influential effect for suburban development were the Home Owners Loan Corporation (HOLC), founded in 1933, and the Federal Housing Administration (FDA), founded in 1934. The HOLC, in short, "[protected] defaulting homeowners against foreclosure"[19] by sending more than $3 billion to regional banks to refinance millions of homes.[20] FHA made it possible even for citizens with low income to buy houses by ensuring that "private capital could flow into the home construction industry"[21]. Although the Depression slowed down the actual progress of suburban construction, the New Deal laid ground for a new standard of American suburban living, as it "put in place an apparatus of financial security that allowed private money to build post-war suburbia"[22].

---

[16] Hayden 2002, p. 50
[17] Baxandall and Ewen 2000, pp. 39-40
[18] Ibid., p. 49
[19] Kennedy, David. "What the New Deal Did". In: *Political Science Quarterly*, Vol. 124, No. 2, 2009, p. 257
[20] Baxandall and Ewen 2000, p. 56
[21] Kennedy 2009, p. 258
[22] Ibid.

The years after the Second World War, particularly the 1950s, marked the most crucial suburban boom in the history of the USA, which resulted from several intertwining phenomena. When the soldiers returned to their mostly young families, there was an "unprecedented demand for affordable housing"[23]. At the same time, the government approved a new kind of compensation that granted money to the veterans only for specific uses, especially for education and homeownership. As a result, although renting would have seemed the safer option, considering the economically bad years of Depression and war, the government encouraged them to help reshaping the American economy by buying homes in suburban areas.[24] Being aware of the newly gained financial potential of returning soldiers, the private housing industry also focused on veteran families as their main target group, often luring them by offering houses for cheap rents in order to eventually transform them into buyers. Both the advertising industry and the national policy portrayed homeownership in the suburbs as the ultimate American way of life, representing not only freedom and independence, but also status and wealth. Post-war suburbanization was furthermore boosted by the increasing popularity of credit financing that came with the end of the Great Depression, which made "purchasing a house seem as easy as buying a toothbrush"[25]. As a consequence, the number of people living in American suburbia rose from 35 million in 1950 to more than 102 million in 1980, and by 1990 more than half of all Americans resided in suburban areas.[26]

In the last three decades, the suburbs have developed into a new urban form, which Robert Fishman calls the "technoburb"[27], a term relating to the significant influence of technological innovations on the modern suburbs, such as the "proliferation of freeways, [...] and the development of sophisticated communication networks"[28]. Whereas in earlier times, people had to commute to their work places which were usually located in the cities, now factories, offices and laboratories offering a range of different jobs are also present in the suburbs. Consequently, these new suburbs are often indistinguishable from the cities. The enormous impact of new technologies is also present in the so called gated communities, a specific private housing option within the framework of suburban structures. The "[desire] for safety, security, community and 'niceness'" is inherent to a lot of American citizens who decide to

---

[23] Kenyon 2004, p.30
[24] Cf. Hayden 2002, p. 54
[25] Baxandall and Ewen 2000, p. 111
[26] Cf. Kenyon 2004, p. 19
[27] Fishman 1987, pp. 190-207
[28] Girling, Cynthia; Helphand, Kenneth. *Yard, Street, Park: The Design of Suburban Open Space.* New York: Wiley 1994, p. 146

live in "secured residential enclaves"[29], predominantly because of the increasing crime rates in both cities and suburbs. As Baxandall and Ewen note, the estimated number of gated communities was 20,000 with about 3 million households in 1997[30], while between 2001 and 2009, the number grew by 53%, leading to "more than 10 million housing units [located] in gated communities"[31] in 2009. The communities are usually protected by private security guards and studded with cameras, leading to full surveillance across the enclosed neighborhoods. Moreover, the residents often have to obey "rigidly enforced rules and regulations"[32] created by the private founders. Despite the significant criticism the founders and inhabitants of gated communities are subject to, the extensive growth of such secured neighborhoods can be regarded as a good indicator of the problems suburban areas are facing today, which I will elaborate on in the course of this book.

2.2 The concept of suburbia as a cultural space

As Bennet Berger already noted in 1962, *suburbia* is not only an "ecological term" that distinguishes suburban areas from cities or the countryside, but at the same time also a "cultural term, intended to connote a way of life"[33]. Berger calls this cultural concept the "suburban myth", as it contains rituals as well as "sacred symbols" and "articles of faith"[34]. According to Berger and others, the visual elements of this myth, which describe the surface structure of suburban landscapes, are the typical T-shaped single-homes with neat front lawns, "winding streets"[35], large garages and picket fences. For Berger, the mythical vision of the suburbs is moreover characterized by homogeneity among its inhabitants, all being in the same range of age, having comparable jobs and sharing a similar family life. Accordingly, suburbia is often imagined as an ideal form of communal living. Other critics, like for example Tom Martinson[36] and Amy Kenyon, call the concept "American dreamscape", making it clear that the landscape of suburbia is particularly linked to and inseparable from America. Combining the connotations of these two terms, *myth* and *dreamscape*, the concept of suburbia can be understood as a sacred but also mysterious and not fully grasped landscape

---

[29] Low, Setha. *Behind the Gates: Life, Security, and the Pursuit of Happiness in Fortress America*. New York: Routledge 2003, pp. 9-10

[30] Baxandall and Ewen 2000, p. 252

[31] Benjamin, Rich. "The Gated Community Mentality". *New York Times Magazine*; March 30, 2012; *New York Time,* p. A27

[32] Baxandall and Ewen 2000, p.252

[33] Berger, Bennet. *Looking for America: Essays on Youth, Suburbia and Other American Obsessions.* Englewood: Prentice Hall 1971, p. 151

[34] Ibid.

[35] Ibid., p. 154

[36] Cf. Martinson, Tom. *American Dreamscape: The Pursuit of Happiness in Postwar Suburbia.* New York: Carroll & Graf Publishers 2000

of the mind. In simpler words, it represents a longing for a better life, a space in which the grass is greener and life is calm and peaceful, "the site of promises, dreams and fantasies"[37]. Kenyon even goes one step further by calling suburbia the "spatialization of the American Dream"[38]. Especially in the era after the Second World War, the central elements of the Dream, like the pursuit of happiness, economic wealth and individual freedom, were all mapped to suburbia, turning the suburbs into America's postwar "Promised Land". The idea/l of suburbia is therefore closely intertwined with both the history and the national identity of America, which makes it possible to legitimately calling it a *cultural* phenomenon.

For the purpose of this book, the most persuasive way to describe suburbia is to call it a cultural *space*, as a space is always both "experienced and created"[39] or, to put it in Michel de Certeau's words, "space is a practiced place"[40]. The term therefore classifies suburbia as the manifestation of the interaction between its physical form and the ideas and visions that people map to it: The space of suburbia does not exist on its own, but is constructed "according to the subject's affective and instrumental relations with it"[41]. It is important to note that the relationship between spaces and the subjects moving in them is interdependent. Not only does the construction of spaces result from the subjects' relations to them, but, as Grosz demonstrates, spatial reference is at the same time important for the subjects' identities: "It is our positioning within space, both as the point of perspectival access to space, and also as an object for others in space, that gives the subject a coherent identity [...] in space"[42].

Returning to the initial discussion of the cultural concept of suburbia, one can conclude that whenever Americans experience suburban living or look at representations of it in literature, art and film, their inner vision of suburbia, culturally informed by the myth or dreamscape explained above, is always actively shaping their perception. For this reason, Kenyon regards the American perspective on suburban existence as "the irresistible spatial arrangement in a culture of avoidance"[43], as people's perception of the suburban space is at all times distorted by a collective nostalgic imagination. She points out that the concept of suburbia is flagged by different layers of detached spaces, for example the one between suburban areas and the city or the detachment caused by the open spaces between suburban

---

[37] Hayden 2003, p. 3
[38] Kenyon 2004, p. 1
[39] Dickinson, Greg. "The Pleasantville Effect: Nostalgia and the Visual Framing of (White) Suburbia". *Western Journal of Communication*, 70, No. 3. (2006), p. 213
[40] De Certeau, Michel. *The Practice of Everyday Life*. Berkeley: University of California Press 1984, p. 117
[41] Grosz, Elizabeth. *Space, Time and Perversion: Essays on the Politics of Bodies*. New York: Routledge 1995, p. 92
[42] Ibid.
[43] Kenyon 2004, p. 45

houses.[44] Following this line of argumentation and combining it with the precedent discussion of *space*, I would argue that the most problematic form of detachment happens on the meta-level, caused by the divergence between today's complex, geographical space of suburbia in the USA and the people's continuous longing for the suburban dream.

As a number of contemporary critics argue, this deviation between the real and the imagined suburban space can be read a logical consequence or byproduct of postmodernism: Dickinson notes that in postmodern America, due to "[massive] migrations, new transportation and communication technologies, and shifting [...] economic and political relations", the physical spaces of the suburban landscape are changing radically, causing "deeply felt anxieties"[45] in suburbanites. Postmodernism, as Fredric Jameson argues, is characterized precisely by "the effacement of some key boundaries or separations"[46]: The same way as the distinction between high culture and mass culture is distorted in postmodernism[47], the fast expansion of suburbia and the transformation into what Fishman calls *technoburbs* can be considered as the collapse of suburbs and cities into one another, thus erasing the reference spaces Americans need to locate themselves within individual and also national identity. Jameson describes this phenomenon as a postmodern dilemma:

> [This] latest mutation in space [...] has finally succeeded in transcending the capacities of the individual human body to locate itself, to organize its immediate surroundings perceptually, and to map cognitively its position in a mappable external world. [This] alarming disjunction between the body and its built environment [...] can itself stand as the symbol and analogue of that even sharper dilemma, which is the incapacity of our minds [...] to map the great global, multinational and decentred communicational network in which we find ourselves caught as individual subjects.[48]

As a reaction to this inability to locate themselves within the quickly transforming physical spaces, individuals try "to create private and public spaces that feel safe"[49] for their better orientation. Concerning the public aspect, the implementation of gated communities can be read as one way to cope with postmodern anxieties, particularly as the gates or walls that fence these planned communities create comprehensible settlements within the otherwise undefined technoburbs. With regard to the private aspect, the individuals' cherishing of the mythical view of suburbia as the American dreamscape can be interpreted as another, psychological way to counteract the postmodern disorientation in space. As I will point out in my analyses of contemporary American movies, this orientation towards the nostalgic space of suburbia functions as an attempt to gain psychological stability, but also leads to further

---

[44] Cf. ibid., pp. 45-68
[45] Dickinson 2004, p. 216
[46] Jameson, Frederic. "Postmodernism and Consumer Society". In: Jameson, Frederic. *The Cultural Turn. Selected Writings on the Postmodern 1983-1998.* London: Verso 1998, p. 2
[47] Ibid.
[48] Ibid., p. 16
[49] Dickinson 2004, p. 216

alienation caused by the strong divergence between the imagined and experienced suburban spaces.

3. Utopian and dystopian narratives of suburbia

As suburbia marks a culturally important and at the same time extremely complex and ambivalent space for Americans, its depiction in fiction is often highly ambiguous as well. Before starting with a detailed analysis of the utopian and dystopian perspectives on suburbia in contemporary American movies, it is necessary to first give a general definition of the concepts of utopia and dystopia as well as an explanation of how these concepts will be used in the further discussion of this book.

The term "utopia" was firstly introduced by the author Sir Thomas More in 1516, when he published his book *Utopia* in which he described an imaginary state on an Atlantic island. Borrowed from Greek, the word utopia is "ambiguous in its derivation"[50], as its origin can be both *ou*-topos, meaning 'no-place', and *eu*-topos, which can be translated as 'good place'. Thus, the term describes an ideal, perfect society does not exist in reality. Accordingly, utopia is a place that is, in Fern's words, "desirable, perhaps, but at the same time unattainable"[51]. The typical utopian narrative tells the story of "a visitor's guided journey through a utopian society which leads to a comparative response that indicts the visitor's own society"[52], providing him[53] with the image of a possible alternative to his own culture. Thus, the relationship between the protagonist's society and the portrayed utopian culture is always significant for the moral of these stories, as the main character always judges the utopian society by the standards that are inherent to the culture he belongs to. Whether the utopian ideal is, in relation to the protagonist, a wishful vision for the future or represents the longing for "[images] of lost paradises and golden ages"[54] of the past, it is always locally separated and distant from his actual society. Therefore, access to this perfect world is usually granted to the protagonist only once, making the experience even more precious and significant.

With regard to the function of the presentation of such a utopian society, giving a comprehensive analysis would certainly go beyond the scope of this book. In Krishan Kumar's opinion, the purpose of utopian fiction is "to overstep the immediate reality to depict a condition whose clear desirability draws us on, like a magnet"[55]. As regards the film analyses to follow, I argue that fictional works on utopia on the one hand criticize the actual culture by showing a perfect society in which the problems found in the real world do not

---

[50] Ferns, Christopher. *Narrating Utopia: Ideology, Gender, Form in Utopian Literature.* Liverpool: Liverpool University Press 1999, p. 2
[51] Ibid.
[52] Baccolini, Raffaella; Moylan, Tom. "Introduction. Dystopia and Histories". In: Baccolini, Raffaella; Moylan, Tom (Eds.). *Dark Horizons: Science Fiction and the Dystopian Imagination.* London: Routledge 2003, p. 5
[53] Most critics agree that the protagonist of the typical utopian story is male.
[54] Levitas, Ruth. "The Archive of the Feet: Memory, Place and Utopia". In: Griffin, Michael; Moylan, Tom (Eds.). *Exploring the Utopian Impulse: Essays on Utopian Thought and Practice.* Peter Lang: Bern 2007, p. 19
[55] Kumar, Krishan. *Utopianism.* Minneapolis: University of Minnesota Press 1991, p. 3

exist. On the other hand, these stories also embrace the actual society in the end, as it is made clear that the utopian culture it is compared to is a mere product of fantasy. For that reason one could regard utopian fiction as both experimental and educational, as it explores possible alternatives to the actual state of being in an abstract and fully imaginary space, while in fact leaving the real society untouched. Within the story, it is the informed visitor who, returning to his own society, can decide how to use the insights gained in utopia, while viewing from the outside, the readers or spectators are invited to critically examine their own society according to the standards presented in the fictional world.

The concept of dystopia can be read as a countermovement to utopian literature, as dystopian fiction openly criticizes the "existing social conditions or political systems"[56]. Whereas utopian fiction explores the differences between the invented and the actual world, the dystopian world is usually depicted as "the nightmare future [being] a possible destination of present society"[57]. The portrayed dystopia can therefore be interpreted as the logical consequence of the deficiencies found in contemporary society. In contrast to most utopian stories, in which the main character travels to the utopian civilization and then returns to his 'real' society as an enlightened individual, the dystopian text "usually begins directly in the terrible new world"[58], focusing on the protagonist's alienation of the dystopian society. In *Film und Utopie*, André Müller notes that the three main topics in dystopian fiction are the function of modern technology as a means of total control over the individual and society in general, the use of biological or psychological manipulation techniques in order to ensure the people's obedience and the citizens' alienated relationship to nature.[59] Accordingly, dystopian fiction draws on the readers' or spectators' anxieties resulting from the nuisances of their actual society, particularly the fear of total control and their loss of individuality. For the subsequent discussion of contemporary American movies, the first motive Müller mentions is the most significant one. As Ferns argues, the "emphasis of on the extraordinarily public character of life"[60] is the common denominator of most popular dystopian works, as the dystopian society is characterized by clear hierarchies and control, forcing its inhabitants to conform to the strict standards it proposes: "[A]ll resources of modern technology are employed to ensure that privacy is kept to an absolute minimum"[61].

---

[56] Booker, Marvin Keith. *Dystopian Literature: A Theory and Research Guide.* Westport: Greenwood Press 1994, p. 3
[57] Ferns 1999, p. 107
[58] Baccolini and Moylan 2003, p. 5
[59] Cf. Müller, André. *Film und Utopie: Positionen des Fiktionalen Films zwischen Gattungstraditionen und Gesellschaftlichen Zukunftsdiskursen.* LIT: Münster 2010, p. 59
[60] Ferns 1999, p. 112
[61] Ferns 1999, p. 113

A number of critics (e.g. Sargent, Moylan) differentiate between the terms *dystopia*, meaning simply the negative of utopia or the ultimate bad place, and *anti-utopia*, often used "to describe those works that use the Utopian form to attack either Utopias in general or a specific Utopia"[62]. Others (e.g. Booker, Ferns) use the term *dystopia* for both phenomena, claiming that "dystopian fiction [combines] a parodic inversion of the traditional utopia with satire on contemporary society"[63]. With regard to the film analyses to follow, I will favor the latter definition of dystopian fiction, thus considering dystopian perspectives as a direct reaction to and criticism of utopian thought. As Gordin, Tilley and Prakash note, dystopia can be considered "utopia's twentieth-century doppelgänger", identifying a "utopia that has gone wrong"[64]. According to this interpretation, any form of dystopia presented in a fictional text is logically dependent on the underlying utopian ideal that is attacked and inversed.

With regard to the depiction of suburbia in American fiction, any utopian portrayal of it is closely connected to the nostalgic, mythical feeling many Americans still have about the suburban space, resulting from its intertwining with the American Dream as discussed above. Thus, a utopian representation of suburbia often focuses on idealized images of the surface structure of suburban neighborhoods, like the integration of nicely built single homes in "uncluttered, contiguous, parklike landscapes", creating the "utopian ideal of perfect community"[65], security and an economically safe life. Many social and literary critics question exactly these virtues, as they consider suburbia rather as a "landscape of mass-produced, uniform tract housing"[66] constituting a "hotbed of conformity"[67]. The dystopian depictions of suburban dwelling in the fictional works to be discussed in the following chapters draw precisely on this criticism, focusing on the destructive forces resulting from the utopian idealization of the suburban space: The utopian view of suburban community, safety and self-realization is inverted in dystopian fiction as it portrays the suburbs as "inauthentic consumption centers and conformity factories"[68], making their residents subject to total control and surveillance.

---

[62] Sargent, Lyman. "The Three Faces of Utopianism Revisited". *Utopian Studies*, Vol. 5, No. 1 (1994), p. 8
[63] Ferns 1999, p. 105
[64] Gordin, Michael; Tilley, Helen; Prakash, Gyan. "Utopia and Dystopia beyond Space and Time". In: Gordin, Michael; Tilley, Helen; Prakash, Gyan (Eds.). *Utopia/Dystopia. Conditions of Historical Possibility*. Princeton: Princeton University Press 2010, p. 1
[65] Beuka 2004, p. 5
[66] Kenyon 2004, p. 72
[67] Beuka 2004, p. 6
[68] Halper and Muzzio 2002, p. 543

4. Suburbia in contemporary American cinema

4.1 Film as narrative space

Before turning to the films to be discussed, it is interesting to first clarify the impact of filmic images of suburbia for the spectator and for society in general. As illustrated in the preceding chapter of this book, suburbia marks a complex and dynamic cultural space that is shaped by the individuals moving in it. As Michel de Certeau argues in his essay "Spatial Stories", narration plays a crucial role in the formation process of spaces, as it is precisely storytelling that creates spaces in the first place[69]. For him, any space is defined (in a mathematical, axiomatic way) by its limitations and interconnections to other spaces, and it is the process of narration that articulates these boundaries:

> "[Where] stories are disappearing, [...] there is a loss of space: deprived of narrations, [...] the group or the individual regresses toward the disquieting, fatalistic experience of a formless indistinct and nocturnal totality. [...] The story's first function is to authorize, or more exactly, to found.[70]

In this sense, one can regard films as a very efficient type of spatial stories, as they are rich cultural texts that combine sight and sound and offer a multisensual experience[71]. In his essay "Narrative Space", Stephen Heath assigns an even more central role to cinematic representations of spaces, claiming that reality itself is "the match of film and world"[72]. By watching movies, according to this interpretation, the spectators actively engage with the spaces perceived on screen by connecting them to their mental images of physical spaces: "[T]he structure of cinematic perception is readily translated into that of natural perception, so much that we can rely on information we construct in viewing films to supplement our common perceptual knowledge"[73]. Coming back to suburban spaces, one can conclude that movies do not merely *depict* suburbia, but that "rather the cinematic images are part and parcel of the ways in which we actually live and act"[74] in it. The establishing shot can be regarded as a simple example of this phenomenon: With the help of this technique, films can show the spectators a landscape, e.g. a suburban neighborhood, from *above*, a perspective they are usually denied in everyday life. Thus in films, as Siegfried Kracauer notes, "many material phenomena which elude observation under normal circumstances"[75] are made visible by methods of perspective, framing and focusing. Be it very small or big things the human

---

[69] De Certeau, Michel. *The Practice of Everyday Life*. Berkeley: University of California Press 1984, p. 123
[70] Ibid., pp. 123-124
[71] Cf. Halper and Muzzio 2002, p. 544
[72] Heath, Stephen. "Narrative Space". In: Rosen, Philip (Ed.). *Narrative, Apparatus, Ideology: A Film Theory Reader*. New York: Columbia University Press 1986, p. 385
[73] Andrew, Dudley: *Concepts in Film Theory*. Oxford, New York: Oxford University Press 1984, p. 41
[74] Dickinson 2004, p. 214
[75] Kracauer, Siegfried. "The Establishment of Physical Existence". In: Braudy, Leo; Cohen, Marshall (Eds.). *Film Theory & Criticism*. Oxford: Oxford University Press 2009, p. 265

eye usually cannot grasp, transitory movement normally unseen or even familiar scenes we do not pay attention to in our everyday life, "films alienate our environment by exposing it"[76]. For these reasons, movies play a significant role in our shaping of suburban spaces. As Burgin states when investigating the space of the city, "[t]he city in our actual experience is *at the same time* an actually existing physical environment, *and* a city in a novel, a film, a photograph, a city seen on television"[77]. To transfer this statement about urban areas onto suburban spaces, one can infer that whenever we actually move in suburbia, our experience is always influenced by the ways in which we have looked and are still looking at the representation of suburbia in movies and art in general. At the same time, when watching suburban movies, our perception of the spaces shown on screen is also filtered by our actual experience of suburbia.

4.2 The invention of reality: Simulations, simulacra, suburbia

As one can conclude from the preceding paragraphs, the mythical or *utopian* concept of suburbia is in a way "immortalized by its simulated representation on television, arts and literature"[78]. It is important to note that the postwar suburbanization of the USA virtually coincided with the entry of television into the American home, so the TV-set was the center of the living room of the typical suburban house. As a consequence, already in the aftermath of the Second World War, TV-shows "provided an illusion of the ideal neighborhood [as just] when people had left their life-long companions in the city, television sitcoms pictured romanticized versions of neighbor and family bonding"[79]. Accordingly, the actual suburban experience was significantly affected by the images of the utopian representations of suburban communities on the television screen already in the 1950s, the time when the idealized concept of suburbia emerged and to which the collective nostalgic imagination is still usually directed to. As a consequence, as Spigel notes, "the lines between electrical and real space"[80] were already distorted in the 1950s. Therefore, it is questionable whether the suburbia shown on screen has indeed ever simulated the actual suburban spaces found in the US, or if it is in fact "'the real' [that] appears as simulation"[81], as Michael Smith states in *Reading Simulacra*. Concerning the impact of television and technology in general in postmodern culture, he

---

[76] Ibid., p. 269
[77] Burgin, Victor. *In-different Spaces: Place and Memory in Visual Culture*. Berkeley, CA: University of California Press 2000, p. 28; His emphasis.
[78] Harvard Law Review (*Author unknown*). "Locating the Suburb". *Harvard Law Review*, Vol. 117, No. 6 (Apr. 2004), p. 2003
[79] Spigel 2001, p. 43
[80] Ibid., p. 44
[81] Smith, Michael. *Reading Simulacra: Fatal Theories for Postmodernity*. Albany: State University of New York Press 2001, p. vii

argues that these innovations "have brought about a new social order in which simulations and models interpenetrate our experiences of the world so deeply that the difference between reality and appearance evaporates"[82]. This statement echoes what Fredric Jameson writes about the collapse of key separations in postmodernism as cited above, and is based on Jean Baudrillard's theoretical approach of simulations and simulacra. Henry Lefebrve argues in a similar way, claiming that "the space born in the second half of the twentieth century is *reproduced* […in] a world of combinations whose every element is known and recognized"[83]. For Baudrillard, America as such is characterized precisely by the fact that reality and fiction, simply speaking, are inseparable: "[American reality] was there before the screen was invented, but everything about the way it is today suggests it was invented with the screen in mind"[84]. Following his definition of simulacra, suburban spaces as portrayed on screen can thus be read as "models of a real without origin or reality: a hyperreal"[85]. Accordingly, following this interpretation, suburbia as an ideological construct has been merely *invented*, and always been imposed by television and other media, in such a way that it seemed *real* for Americans. While sitcoms of the postwar period enforced this suburban ideal by presenting the nuclear family and perfect neighborhood as the norm, many postmodern texts challenge this view by revealing the very fictionality of the mystified suburban space. In the succeeding film analyses, this postmodern theory of suburbia as simulacrum will be discussed more closely.

4.3 Suburbia as setting and center of contemporary American Films: Introduction to the film analyses

As living in the suburbs is the standard for most US citizens, it is no surprise that the portrayal of suburbia is found in a great number of contemporary American movies and TV-series. The continuing success of series like *Weeds* (2005-today), *Desperate Housewives* (2004-2012) and *The Simpsons* (1989-today) give proof of the ongoing public interest in critical cinematic representations of suburban existence. At the close of the twentieth century, several commercially very successful movies focused on the problems associated with life in American suburbia, as for instance *SuBurbia* (1996), *Ice Storm* (1997), *Happiness* (1998), as well as the movies to be analyzed in the course of this book, namely *Pleasantville* (1998), *The Truman Show* (1998) and *American Beauty* (1999).

---

[82] Ibid.
[83] Lefebrve, Henri; Moore, Gerald (Transl.); Brenner, Neil (Ed.); Elden, Stuart (Ed.). *State, Space, World. Selected Essays.* Minneapolis: University of Minnesota Press 2009, pp. 212-13; Emphasis added.
[84] Baudrillard, Jean. *America.* New York: Verso 1989, p. 55
[85] Baudrillard, Jean. *Simulacra and Simulation.* Michigan: Mich. University Press 2010, p. 1

As Halper and Muzzio argue, one can distinguish between films that are merely located in an American suburb and those that center on suburbia as the central narrative space[86]. Particularly the last three films mentioned above are not only "set in a suburb for all or a major part of the action" but also focus on suburban life in a way that the stories "could not take place elsewhere without being fundamentally altered"[87]. The common denominator uniting *Pleasantville*, *The Truman Show* and *American Beauty* concerning their contents is the focus on the male protagonists' search for an alternative to their dysfunctional suburban existence. In this way, the movies draw on the collective postmodern anxieties discussed above, particularly by exploring the "craving for authenticity [against] the artificiality and shallowness of the reality"[88]. As a consequence, the films all share different realizations and at the same time criticisms of the "Nostalgia mode"[89], as the longing for a distant, safer or more authentic past is central to all of them: Both *Pleasantville* and *The Truman Show* employ a "1950s'-style suburban situation comedy as a metaphor for exploring the repressions and assorted neuroses of contemporary American suburbia"[90] while Lester, the protagonist of *American Beauty,* feeling confined and repressed in his seemingly perfect suburban life, tries to escape the dystopian space by returning to his teenager alter ego. Concerning their shared cinematic devices, the films focus on suburbia by different means of multi-layered mediation, "placing the audience at a distance from the impossibilities the films proffer"[91]. In *Pleasantville*, the action takes place in a TV-show within the film, while in *The Truman Show*, the viewers' function is even more confusing, as they are at the same time spectators of the "Truman Show" within the movie and of *The Truman Show* itself. Although *American Beauty* does not take up this obvious fiction-within-fiction style, the director makes use of various other distanciation effects, like the protagonist's posthumous voice-over-narration and the presentation of parts of the action through the lenses of the video camera of one of the characters. The impact of modern technology and surveillance on suburban existence is also a central topic in these three movies and will be discussed thoroughly. By providing a close reading of these three films throughout the following chapters, I will examine and compare the different utopian and dystopian views of suburbia they portray as postmodern texts and explore their central criticism of the suburban ideal.

---

[86] Halper and Muzzio 2002, p. 547
[87] Ibid.
[88] Fitting, Peter. "Unmasking the Real? Critique and Utopia in Recent SF Films". In: Baccolini, Raffaella; Moylan, Tom (Eds.). *Dark Horizons: Science Fiction and the Dystopian Imagination.* London: Routledge 2003, p. 158
[89] Beuka 2004, p. 229
[90] Ibid., p. 228
[91] Dickinson 2004, p. 227

5. Once upon a time: Suburbia as nostalgic utopia in *Pleasantville*

5.1 Introduction and plot summary

In *Pleasantville*, published in 1998, Gary Ross criticizes the collective nostalgia regarding the suburban ideal of the 1950s by satirically questioning its validity as a utopian construct. As Kumar argues, the essence of utopia is the desire "[to] live in a world that cannot be but where one fervently wishes to be"[92]. This is precisely the feeling that can be ascribed to David, the teenage main character of *Pleasantville*: Living with his twin sister Jennifer and his single mother in a suburban neighborhood somewhere in the south of the USA, he is alienated and depressed by both his torn family and school life. He therefore compensates his desire for more stability by regularly watching a black-and-white TV-show called "Pleasantville"[93], set in a romantic and neat suburban neighborhood and focusing on the simple but happy life of a 1950s nuclear family. An apparent television repairman hands the teenagers a special remote control, by the use of which David and Jennifer are magically drawn into the TV-show to find themselves in the roles of Bud and Mary-Sue Parker, the children of the family on which the show focuses. In Pleasantville, life seems perfectly ordered, safe and sterile for them. There is no poverty, no hunger, no prejudice or hate, even fire and rain are not found in this apparently utopian environment. But despite his initial longing to be transported into Pleasantville, David gradually follows his sister by "intuitively and explicitly [railing] against the sanitized, claustrophobic, even authoritarian, atmosphere of a town that has no access to information concerning what is beyond itself"[94]. The twins introduce their knowledge of sexuality and culture to the citizens of "Pleasantville", which turns their lives upside down: Step by step, both the newly enlightened citizens and their environment become colored, while the older, mostly male citizens who stick to the rules and traditional values remain in black-and-white. As a consequence, the conservatives try to restrain their fellow citizens from gaining more knowledge while at the same time effectively banishing the newly colored people from stores and public buildings. At the end, David is put on a trial and has to defend himself in front of all citizens in the courthouse of Pleasantville. He succeeds in convincing even the conservatives of the importance of freedom and individuality, which finally transforms Pleasantville in a fully colorful place. While David

---

[92] Kumar 1991, p. 1

[93] In the following, I will refer to the film in italicized letters (*Pleasantville*) and to the TV-show by using quotation marks ("Pleasantville"). When talking about the suburb depicted on screen, I will refer to it as Pleasantville (non-italicized and without quotation marks).

[94] Porter, Robert. "Habermas in Pleasantville: Cinema as Political Critique". *Contemporary Political Theory*, 13.2 (2007), p. 410

leaves Pleasantville and returns to his actual home at the end of the film, his sister Jennifer stays in the fictional world.

5.2 The opening scenes: Real vs. nostalgic visions of suburbia

Already at the beginning of *Pleasantville*, Gary Ross introduces the two realms of the film, namely the complex and confusing life in American suburbia of the late twentieth century and the idealized suburban life of the 1950s sitcom "Pleasantville" by contrasting them in the opening scenes. In the first sequence of the film, a short TV-preview for the "Pleasantville" marathon is employed which introduces the black-and-white sitcom to the spectators of the film even before the actual story begins. The preview depicts the orderly suburban structure of Pleasantville as it shows a shiny, huge and symmetrical T-shaped house from outside before cutting to an establishing shot of the neighborhood. All houses are associated with stereotypical large and neatly trimmed front yards, lined with bushes of roses and framed by white picket fences, a portrayal that includes all elements of the iconic "visual vocabulary of the suburb"[95], as Dickinson argues. The spectators are then introduced to the Parkers, who function as the main characters of the show. One can see that gender roles are clearly defined in "Pleasantville", as Betty is waiting for her husband George to come home from work after having already prepared dinner in the kitchen for him and their children. Ross employs a range of long shots with no or only little movement which underscore the impression of stability and peacefulness that is produced by the action taking place on screen.

After the preview, the actual film starts with a series of quick shots portraying high school students moving across a school courtyard in contemporary America, a close-up of a girl playing with her tongue piercing and very short shots depicting various cliques gathering on the yard. The dynamic camera movements and the hustle shown on screen stand in direct opposition to the static shots of the Pleasantville preview, which makes the scenes appear hectic and threatening. David, the main character of the film, is then shown in a close-up while he is apparently flirting with a very pretty girl. Both of them are filmed alternately in reverse-angle shots while David is talking to her stammeringly, before the camera cuts to an extreme long shot, in which the spectator sees that David and the girl are in fact standing about 100 feet away from each other. Accordingly, this scene portrays communication and personal relationships as difficult to achieve nowadays, which contrasts extremely to the simple and clear chats between the characters of "Pleasantville". This impression of the

---

[95] Dickinson 2004, p. 219

"complexity of life in the late twentieth century"[96] is further strengthened in the next scenes that take the spectator inside several classrooms, where the students are warned by their teachers about their bad job prospects, venereal diseases, AIDS, global warming, famine and other probable catastrophes.[97]

When Ross introduces David's neighborhood for the first time, the camera follows a Westec[98] patrol car driving slowly through a completely empty and lifeless suburban area[99], from which one can infer that his family lives in a gated community. Thus, even though the houses and lots look similarly appealing as those in the preview of "Pleasantville" on first sight, the presence of the watchmen and the fact that nobody is seen on the streets indicate the potential danger of crime and at the same time evoke the feeling of synthetic entrapment and surveillance in the spectators. In an early version of the script of *Pleasantville*, one can see that Ross wanted to achieve an even more depressing effect:

> **EXT. WAGNER HOUSE. DUSK.**
> It is a south-western version of "Leave it to Beaver." The uniformity of Suburbia has been washed in earth tones. There   is a red tile roof gracing every home. All the houses have the same anemic palm tree. It's an urban planner's version of hell.[100]

As this establishing shot directly follows after the disturbing scenes at the high school, the contemporary problems mentioned by the teachers are virtually mapped to the suburban landscape. Ironically, this exterior shot is accompanied by the theme music of "Pleasantville", a parallelization which one can read as a satiric comment on the obvious "differences between present suburbia and nostalgically held TV memories of 1950s suburbia"[101]. Ross goes one step further when he contrasts David's shattered family life to the supposedly wholesome and stable one of the "Pleasantville" characters by means of juxtaposition in the next scenes. While David's mother is fighting to her ex-husband on the phone about child custody, David watches the Parkers on TV while they are talking warm-heartedly at dinner. Ross alternately presents the spectator scenes from "Pleasantville" and shots from the inside of David's house, showing him sitting on the couch and his mother running up and down the bedroom while shouting into the phone. Obviously, the comparison of the two mothers is central to this scene:

---

[96] Reinhartz, Adele. *Scripture on the Silver Screen.* Louisville: Westminster John Know Press 2003, p. 146
[97] Cf. Fitting 2003, p. 162
[98] Westec Intelligent Surveillance, Inc. is an American company providing video surveillance solutions for companies across the USA. See http://www.westec.net/
[99] See figure 1
[100] See http://www.imsdb.com/scripts/Pleasantville.html
[101] Dickinson 2004, p. 218

DAVID'S MOM
No, that's not the point Barry. You're supposed to see them. Fine, fine, fine. See them   another time.
DAVID (quietly)
What's a mother to do?
BETTY (on T.V. looking right into the camera)
Oh--what's a mother to do?[102]

Whereas according to the telephone conversation, David's mother seems to regard her children as a burden, Betty is portrayed as the perfect mother and housewife. David's yearning gaze and the fact that he knows the characters' lines by heart clearly indicate his longing for a stable family life like the one he perceives when watching his favorite TV-show.

As a result of this extreme comparison of the two different suburban worlds in the opening scenes, the spectators "are expected to endorse that negative view of contemporary America" on the one hand, and at the same time invited to share the protagonist's longing for travelling to "a simpler America in the 1950s"[103]. This way, Pleasantville is immediately presented as a form of nostalgic utopian landscape, incorporating the traditional family values that are apparently missing nowadays.

5.3 The utopia of *Pleasantville*

As pointed out in the third chapter of this book, the typical utopian narrative focuses on a character's guided journey to a utopian society and ends with his return to his own world as an informed visitor. Regarding this essential narrative framework, *Pleasantville* can definitely be considered a utopian story. Even the name of "Pleasantville", meaning basically 'good city', is a synonym of the term *utopia (eu-topia)*. Moreover, as the film alludes to the fact that there are numerous Pleasantvilles found across the USA, the spectators get the impression that this ideal society could be found everywhere potentially, although it still remains a fictional, not mappaple no-place (*ou-topia*). This corresponds to Kumar's understanding, as he argues that every type of "[utopia] distinguishes itself from other forms of the ideal society [...] by being in the first place a piece of fiction"[104]. By the insertion of an intertitle saying "Once upon a time..." before the actual film starts, Ross makes it clear from the very beginning that not only the utopian society of Pleasantville is completely fictional, but also the whole story of the movie, which is a mere fairytale. Because of this elaborate form of mediation, the spectators are restrained from identifying too intensely with the characters and actions depicted on screen, and are instead invited to critically analyze the utopian narrative.

---

[102] *Pleasantville*, TC 00:05:22
[103] Gallardo, Pere. "The Road to Perdition is Paved in Technicolour". In: Russell, Elizabeth (Ed.).
Trans/Forming Utopia: The 'Small Thin Story'. Bern: Peter Lang 2009, p. 218
[104] Kumar 1991, p. 20

Typically for a utopian society, Pleasantville is isolated from the protagonist's society by means of an intricate combination of time and location. According to the TV repairman, access to this utopia is granted only to very special people, as only "those who truly long to live in this idealized world are eligible"[105]: "You look for someone for years, you pour your heart into it... This is a privilege, you know"[106]. David cannot simply travel to Pleasantville because he wishes to do so, but instead is *chosen* by a higher authority, or God-figure, which already hints at the religious allusions found in *Pleasantville*.

By contrasting the two suburban realms of the 1950s sitcom and America of the 1990s, the director illustrates the tension between the utopian, nostalgic ideal of suburbia and the real, contemporary suburban space which he develops in the course of the film. The utopia of Pleasantville is thus created through the comparison with the defective present society, as the fictional world offers a possible alternative to the problems depicted in the real world. In terms of suburban dwelling, the postwar period marks a kind of Golden Age for Americans for numerous reasons already illustrated in the previous chapters. More specifically, the suburban utopia of *Pleasantville* stands for the 1950s "not as this era was in reality but as it is represented in the media"[107]. As Kumar notes, "[virtually] all societies have some myth or memory of Golden Age", a time "of simplicity and sufficiency"[108]. The suburban space of Pleasantville therefore works so well as a model of utopia because it draws on the American spectators' inherent nostalgia or "yearning for return [despite the] ambivalent recognition that such is not possible"[109].

5.4 Exploring utopia: The suburban space of Pleasantville

Some of the visual components or "suburban aesthetics"[110], like for instance the typical T-shaped houses and large front yards that define the suburban space of Pleasantville have already been addressed in the previous paragraph. The single houses are detached, as the white picket fences and driveways separate one property from the next one. Pleasantville is moreover characterized by the separation of "residential space from commercial and civic space"[111], as on Elm Street, all the inhabitants' houses are located, whereas on Main Street, one finds the Soda Shop, the Barber Shop and the Town Hall, but no houses. Because of the

---

[105] Mercadante, Linda. "The God Behind the Screen: *Pleasantville* & *The Truman Show*". *Journal of Religion and Film*, Vol. 5, No. 2 (October 2001), p. 3
[106] *Pleasantville*, TC 00:14:41
[107] Reinhartz 2003, p. 150
[108] Kumar 1991, p. 4
[109] Davis, Fred. *Yearning for Yesterday: A Sociology of Nostalgia*. New York: Free Press 1979, p. 21
[110] Dickinson 2004, p. 218
[111] Ibid., p. 219

spacious yards and the numerous trees framing the streets, one gets the idea of a neat symbiosis of nature and dwelling spaces that reminds the informed spectator of the early visions of suburban landscaping promoted by architects like Olmsted, Beecher and Downing.[112] The beautiful, even Edenic outline of the garden at Lover's Lane underscores the impression of Pleasantville as Paradise.

In terms of the citizens' way of life, the central features that define the suburban space of Pleasantville are its simplicity and stability. As the spectators find out when watching David and Jennifer explore Pleasantville, the inhabitants' lives are characterized by the repetition of everyday routines: Women basically spend their whole day in the kitchen, being mainly responsible for preparing hearty breakfasts and dinners for their working husbands and children. High school students spend their leisure time either in the town's Soda Shop or at Lover's Lane, where boys and girls go for holding hands. Men leave the house in the morning for work – although the spectator never actually sees them at their work places – and return at night to enjoy dinner with their families. These routines are found in every possible aspect of life in Pleasantville: The weather is always sunny with mild 72 degrees, the school's basketball team is undefeated because every shot magically finds the basket, and the only raison d'être of the local fire brigade is to save cats out of trees, as nothing burns in the suburb. Even physical needs are not present in Pleasantville, as the citizens are completely unaware of their sexuality and basic bodily functions. The cabins in the restrooms are empty, as there is simply no need for toilets. The apparent perfectness of Pleasantville, one might argue, is thus achieved through absolute predictability and the total lack of dangers, risks and variations.

Consequently, Pleasantville can be considered as a completely static suburban space at the beginning of the film. This fact is also visualized on screen, particularly in the scene in which Ross presents the spectator a geography lesson in the high school, when the teacher shows the students a drawn map of Pleasantville, consisting of only two streets and the town hall.[113] As the audience finds out, the students are taught that there is nothing outside of Pleasantville:

JENNIFER
What's outside of Pleasantville?
MISS PETERS
What? I don't understand...
JENNIFER
Outside of Pleasantville ... What's at the end of Main Street?
MISS PETERS
Oh, Mary Sue. You should know the answer to that. The end of Main Street is just the beginning again.[114]

---

[112] See Chapter 2
[113] See figure 2
[114] *Pleasantville*, TC 00:21:30

This situation shown on screen once more makes it clear to the spectators that the citizens of Pleasantville live in a hermeneutical circle, with no knowledge at all of places beyond the border of Pleasantville. For all these reasons, the seemingly utopian space of Pleasantville appears more and more ridiculous to the spectators in the course of the film. If one considers Pleasantville as a symbol of "Americans' hunger for nostalgia"[115], one can interpret this overstated depiction of the 1950s suburb as a "critique of the ideological fantasy of small-town America"[116] and the mythical concept of suburbia. What seems like a desirable alternative to the contemporary society on first sight, simply turns out to be "not acceptable for "real life""[117]. As already discussed before, spaces are dynamic concepts, always changing and constantly being recreated by the subjects moving in them, which is precisely the reason for the fall of Pleasantville in its static version.

5.5 The creation of new spaces in Pleasantville

Although David initially endorses the stability and safety of Pleasantville and tries to convince his sister of the importance to play along with the everyday routines, he soon realizes that he cannot stop the transformation of Pleasantville. As Porter argues, the twins introduce "two elements into the social body [of Pleasantville]: sexuality and culture"[118]. While Jennifer tells and shows her fellow students about sex, David shares his knowledge of art and literature with the citizens of the suburb, which literally "[shakes] the Pleasantville world order to its very core"[119]: Gradually, "fragments of color begin to appear in various places"[120], first on flowers and items like cars and bubble gums and later also individual people are shown in Technicolor, while others remain in black-and-white at first. Moreover, the furniture store suddenly sells double beds and the jukeboxes play Rock'n'Roll songs that did not exist in Pleasantville before. What the spectator witnesses is precisely the transformation of *space* of Pleasantville, as one can read the various visual signs of change as material manifestations of the recreation of space in the fictional 1950s suburb. As pointed out above, stories play a significant role in the dynamic formation of spaces, a fact that Ross literalizes visibly on screen when David tells his friends the tale of Huckleberry Finn: As soon as David recounts the story while holding the book in his hands, the blank pages become magically filled with letters and images, which symbolizes the extension of general

---

[115] Halper and Muzzio 2002, p. 549
[116] Fitting 2003, p. 162
[117] Dickinson 2004, p. 221
[118] Porter 2007, p. 410
[119] Reinhartz 2003, p. 150
[120] Ibid.

knowledge in Pleasantville, and also the broadening of the citizens' horizons. This phenomenon echoes Michel de Certeau's words, as he claims that "[the story] has distributive power and performative force [...] when an ensemble of circumstances is brought together. Then it founds spaces"[121]. But David does not only teach his fellow students about literature, he moreover tells them that there is a world beyond Pleasantville:

> **MARGARET**
> What's outside of Pleasantville?
> **DAVID**
> Well ... There are some places where the road doesn't go in a circle. There are some places where it keeps on going.
> **GIRL**
> Keeps going ...
> **DAVID**
> Yeah, it keeps going. Well, it all just keeps going. Roads ... rivers ...[122]

As a consequence, the geographical space of Pleasantville also expands after a while, which is demonstrated by the appearance of road signs indicating directions to places outside the suburb. Storytelling, one can conclude, is shown as the starting point to form new spaces in the film.

Of course, it is not solely narration that leads to the alteration of space in Pleasantville, but also the inhabitants' inner, psychological change. As a result of Jennifer's and David's influence, the citizens begin to think outside the box and question their rigid way of life: At first it is only the high school students who start to have sex and to develop an appetite for more knowledge which is shown by their rush to the library. After some time, however, this change is also found in the adult citizens of Pleasantville, particularly in Betty and Mr. Johnson who fall in love with each other and also consume their relationship. As a result, more and more individuals and also places like Lover's Lane and the Soda Shop turn into color, which demonstrates the people's power to influence and shape the space in which they are living. According to Henri Lefebvre, "a new space cannot be born (produced) unless it accentuates differences"[123]. Thus the appearance of Technicolor, in simple words, can be interpreted as the most dominant sign of the creation of new spaces, especially as the use of color opposes the static and monochrome to the dynamic and multichrome aspects of space in Pleasantville. Accordingly, Ross uses colors as the central mark of change, which seems to be closely tied to the citizens' sexual awakening on first sight: The first piece of color appears on a red rose after Jennifer has seduced her boyfriend in Lover's Lane for the first time, and Betty becomes 'colored' after she has masturbated in the bath tub. In the course of the film,

---

[121] De Certeau 1984, p. 123

[122] *Pleasantville*, TC 00:50:24

[123] Lefebvre, Henri. Nicholson-Smith, Donald (Trans.). *The Production of Space*. Oxford: Blackwell 1991.

however, it is made clear that the colors are not exclusively connected to sexuality, especially as Jennifer remains black and white although she has more sex than anyone else in Pleasantville. She turns into color after her decision to give preference to studying, while David becomes colored after having defended Betty against a group of boys who try to assault her, thus bringing violence to the town for the first time. David's change in this scene can be read as the closure of his journey to himself in Pleasantville, and also as a symbolic reunification with his (real) mother. He now seems to embrace the idea that life cannot be perfect and stable, but that all people naturally have a dark side inside them: Passion and devotion, as the film shows, are inseparable from anger and violence. One can therefore infer that color is used to depict a profound change of the mind in the characters, an opening up for repressed feelings and desires, i.e. an enrichment of their psychological, individual spaces.

5.6 The end of paradise: Fall of Man, racism and visions of dystopia

The creation of new spaces in Pleasantville is not entirely positive, since it also brings unknown disturbances to the citizens, as "[r]elationships end, the weather gets worse, choice and risks are introduced, confusion and pain set in"[124]. If one considers the constancy of the fictional 1950s suburb as the central feature of its utopian character, the transformation initiated by David and Jennifer undoubtedly marks the end of the utopian society. As Gallardo notes: "[i]n most utopian and dystopian texts, any kind of external interference eventually implies the destruction or implosion of the system"[125].

Ross displays the destruction of utopia mainly by means of religious analogy to the biblical Fall of Man. The major events that lead to the final transformation of Pleasantville, namely Betty's move-out and her first sexual contact with Mr. Johnson, Jennifer's intense study experience and the first thunderstorm that hits the suburb all happen at the day when David takes Margaret to Lover's Lane for the first time. According to Richard Armstrong, "colour and desire become equated" in the scene in which the couple drives to the park area, as they find themselves "amid billows of pink cherry blossom petals"[126], which makes the park area a perfect replication of the Garden of Eden. This impression is underscored when they finally arrive at the lake, as the whole area is shiny and colorful, with young people sitting at the waterside and reading to each other. The most significant scene that sums up all

---

[124] Mercadante 2001, p. 4
[125] Gallardo 2009, p. 223
[126] Armstrong, Richard. "'Where Am I Going to See Colours Like That?' Bliss, Desire and the Paintbox in Pleasantville". *Screen Education,* No. 52 (2008), p. 158

the actions mentioned above that are juxtaposed in the film takes place at night, when David
and Margaret are sitting at the waterside and talking about the world outside Pleasantville:

MARGARET
So what's it like?
DAVID
What?
MARGARET
Out there.
DAVID
Well it's louder ... And scarier I guess ... And, it's a lot more dangerous...
MARGARET
Sounds fantastic.[127]

In this scene, one can already read the connection between knowledge and sexuality that
unites all the events mentioned above. After this conversation, Margaret gets up to pluck a
shiny and red ripe apple and offers it seductively to David, in a way that obviously reminds
the spectators of Adam and Eve and the biblical image of temptation. According to Reinhartz,
this scene therefore represents the "expulsion from the garden, the onset of mortality and the
initiation of human life and history as we know it"[128]. The exclusion from Paradise, or in this
case the destruction of utopia, is thus shown to be the necessary cost for knowledge, sexuality
and individuality.

While a lot of citizens of Pleasantville embrace the ongoing transformation of space, the
conservative group, including the mayor and a number of mostly male citizens, show a strong
desire to return things back to the original stability and order. In an official assembly at the
town hall, they consequently agree upon a Code of Conduct that forbids any innovation in the
town, including the reading of books, usage of colors other than black, white and grey, and
listening to Rock'n'Roll music. At the same time, the newly colored citizens become subject
to hatred and segregation and are banished from public places like stores and the town hall.
As Beuka argues, at this point, the film shows that "suburban homogeneity equals dangerous
cultural conformity"[129], as the spectators witness that "conservatism slides into
authoritarianism"[130] in Pleasantville, which demonstrates that the line between utopia and
dystopia is very thin in fact. As Ferns argues,

"in suppressing the emergence of individual identity in the interests of stability, security, conformity,
the dystopian state clearly seeks to discourage the development of any kind of mature, adult awareness
– of any form of consciousness sophisticated enough to perceive and articulate the society's
limitations".[131]

---

[127] *Pleasantville*, TC 01:08:38
[128] Reinhartz 2003, p. 152
[129] Beuka 2004, p. 235
[130] Porter 2007, p. 410
[131] Ferns 1999, p. 114

According to this definition, Pleasantville is about to become a fully dystopian state at this point of the movie. One could even go one step further by claiming that it has always been rather dystopian than utopian, as the seemingly perfect world has at all times been an illusion masking "repressed emotions, cardboard personalities, stale and static relationships and, more insidiously, hatred of change and of difference"[132]. The transformation of space in Pleasantville thus ultimately unmasks the seemingly paradisiacal order as a "ridiculous dictate"[133].

In terms of cinematic techniques, Ross strengthens this sense of dystopia by the employment of extensive zooming, fast cutting and distorted angles, which stand in strong opposition to the stable long shots from the beginning of the film. No matter how threatening these shots appear, however, they also function as another means of expansion of the space of Pleasantville, which one can see best in the scene in which Betty is attacked by the group of youngsters. In this scene, Ross uses a handheld camera for the first time, which evokes a feeling of chaos and danger on the one hand, but on the other also creates a very naturalistic effect. When the camera then circles around Betty showing her in a near 360-degree-shot, it seems like Ross introduces another dimension to the suburban space of Pleasantville, as what seemed flat and artificial at the beginning now appears three-dimensional and real. Again, the spectator is shown that dangers and risks belong to everyday life and that they help to enrich spaces rather than destroying them.

The affirmation of the imperfection of life seems to be the general tenor at the end of *Pleasantville*. In the court scene, Ross finally dissolves the tension between the utopian and dystopian impulse, as Pleasantville is turned into full color including the conservatives, as a result of David's summation:

DAVID
I know you want it to stay "pleasant" around here, but there are so many things that are so much better: like silly ... or sexy ... or dangerous... or brief.
And every one of those things is in you all the time if you just have the guts to look for them.[134]

Consequently, the suburban space of Pleasantville resembles reality a lot at the end of the film. The fact that David returns to his old life despite his success in the fictional world demonstrates that he now recognizes the discomforts of contemporary American suburban life as a central ingredient of his being. "Instead of attempting to escape", as Fitting argues, David finally "acknowledge[s] and confront[s] the dystopian aspects of the present"[135] and even appreciates the dynamic essence of the spaces that characterize his existence. When he is

---

[132] Reinhartz 2003, p. 158
[133] Porter 2007, p. 410
[134] *Pleasantville*, TC 01:39:40
[135] Fitting 2003, p. 164

united with his real mother in the end, the way he gently wipes the tears out of her face strongly reminds the spectator of the scene in which he applies grey make-up on Betty, which parallels the two women to another, implying that David's longing for a different and more stable family life is over and that he can now accept his mother's flaws as part of what he loves about her.

5.7 Happy ever after? A summarizing reading of *Pleasantville*

Although at the beginning of the film, *Pleasantville* portrays the contemporary American suburban space as dystopian and threatening, it embraces its complexity including all its dangers and merits in the end by revealing that the utopian vision of postwar suburbia is shallow and completely devoid of any relation to real life. As the film "draws on memory to imagine the good life in suburbia"[136], it criticizes Americans' collective nostalgia by unmasking the utopian visions of the 1950s suburban existence as "realities […] that where served up in the family sitcoms of the era"[137]. In simple words, this implies that the ideal suburbia people are still longing for today has always only existed in TV-series and never in reality. Throughout the movie, Ross demonstrates that the slightest influence from the real world leads to the implosion of the static space of suburban utopia, precisely due to its superficial and fake character. As Pleasantville is not fully destroyed in the end but changed for the better, the film still does not argue against nostalgia, but for a version of "a nostalgia that is leavened with a hint of danger or risk [that] leads to full human emotions"[138]. Ross shows that the stability of Pleasantville is only possible by means of suppression of any form of individualism and by segregating those that lean against the authoritarian power of the leaders. In fact, the director mirrors parts of the history of the USA in *Pleasantville*, as the banishment of the coloreds clearly "entails the very visible and obvious overtones of the civil rights strife in the United States of the 1950s"[139], while the beginning emancipation of the town's female citizens moreover reminds the audience of the sexual revolution that took place between 1960 and 1980. These relations to real historic events achieves effects that are significant for the understanding of American suburbia as a cultural space: Ross demonstrates that the postwar period, which is idealized by many Americans still today, had numerous deficits that eventually led to quarrels and revolutions to change society for the better. Therefore, Ross makes the spectators critically revise their image of this presumably ideal

---

[136] Dickinson 2004, p. 218
[137] Reinhartz 2003, p. 158
[138] Dickinson 2004, p. 222
[139] Ibid., p. 159

period and their vision of postwar suburbia as a utopia. The suburban space of contemporary America is thus affirmed in the film, and shown to be the logical consequence of a historical development that was necessary in terms of freedom and self-realization of individuals.

6. Better than reality? Suburbia as simulacra in *The Truman Show*

6.1 Introduction and plot summary

In his popular and highly successful film *The Truman Show*, published in 1998, Peter Weir sharply satirizes the utopian ideal of postwar suburbia by portraying the suburban space as mere simulacra and "as a landscape of imprisonment and control"[140]. The movie depicts the last episodes of a reality-TV program which is also called "The Truman Show"[141] and focuses on the everyday life of the thirty-year old insurance agent Truman Burbank, who has been filmed for all of his life without knowing it. He is the only star of the series that is broadcasted live 24/7 all over the world, as in contrast to him, all the other characters of the show know about the artificiality of his life. His wife, family and friends are merely actors getting paid for keeping up the illusion of reality to him, and the neighborhood in which he has spent all his life is in fact a gigantic studio dome located in Hollywood and controlled by the show's creator Christof and a production team. In 'Seahaven Island', a picturesque 1950s-style suburb, the producer even simulates daytimes and weather changes and monitors every single movement of Truman with more than 5,000 hidden cameras spread all over the dome. The story sets in when Truman witnesses one of the studio's spotlights falling down and landing in front of his house, which marks the beginning of his skepticism towards his environment. Being alarmed by this incidence, Truman notices more and more irregularities in his everyday life and surroundings, like his wife's obvious way of advertising various products at their home or that some people in his neighborhood move in loops, periodically appearing at the same places over and over again. Throughout the film, Truman becomes more and more paranoid and determined to find out the truth about his existence. His attempts to free himself "are met by correspondingly frantic efforts on the parts of Christof and his crew to keep Truman in ignorance and on Seahaven"[142], but he nevertheless succeeds in escaping his suburban home one night without the producer's notice to leave the town by boat, which leads to the first temporary interruption in the show's history. Despite Christof's various efforts to stop him, like the employment of a severe thunderstorm that nearly leads to Truman's death by drowning, the latter finally reaches the edge of the studio system. Although Christof tries to convince Truman of the privilege to live inside the realm of the TV-show by talking personally to him for the first time through loudspeakers, the film ends after Truman has left the studio via a side exit door.

---

[140] Beuka 2004, p. 227

[141] In the following, I will refer to the film in italicized letters (*The Truman Show*) and to the show within the film by using quotation marks ("The Truman Show").

[142] Reinhartz 2003, p. 8

6.2 Different layers of diegesis: Utopian and dystopian perspectives in *The Truman Show*

As Peter Marks notes in his essay "Imagining Surveillance: Utopian Visions and Surveillance Studies", *The Truman Show* marks "a test case for the complex relationship between utopias and dystopias"[143]. On the one hand, Truman's world could be considered as utopia, as he has spent the first thirty years of his life in a stable, happy and completely secure way, in a space free of real dangers and the deeply felt anxieties people are facing in contemporary suburban America. In this way, Seahaven resembles Pleasantville a lot, as it is "always sunny, always clean, and conspicuously free from the social ills of poverty and homelessness"[144]. One could thus regard Truman as a privileged traveler living in a utopian society, as he is the only one who is given the chance to live in a world that many Americans long for. On the other hand, topics such as the impact of modern technology, mass media and the use of surveillance measures to keep Truman unaware of the artificiality of his world are central to the movie. Moreover, if one considers the typical dystopian narrative, which in contrast to the guided voyage in utopian narratives "places us directly in a dark and depressing reality"[145] and focuses on the protagonist's estrangement of the depicted society, one can clearly call *The Truman Show* a dystopian story.

Within the film, the question whether to regard Truman's suburban world as utopian or dystopian comes out most clearly in the discussion between Christof, the creator of "The Truman Show", and Silvia, who had been a cast member once and is a strong opponent of the show:

> **SILVIA**
> What right do you have to take a baby and turn his life into some kind of mockery? Don't you ever feel guilty?
>
> **CHRISTOF**
> I have given Truman a chance to lead a normal life. The world, the place *you* live in, is the sick place. Seahaven's the way the world should be.[146]

If one neglects the philosophical questions of truth and knowledge that are certainly central to the discussion of *The Truman Show* but cannot be tackled satisfyingly within the scope of this book, the tension between utopian and dystopian perspectives is mostly a result of the intricate narrative structure: As Dietmar Kammerer notes in *Bilder der Überwachung*, the film combines three planes of diegesis, namely the one of the film itself, the one of the TV-

---

[143] Marks, Peter. "Imagining Surveillance: Utopian Visions and Surveillance Studies". *Surveillance & Society*, 3 (2005), p. 228
[144] Reinhartz 2003, p. 9
[145] Gordin, Tilley and Prakash 2010, p. 2
[146] *The Truman Show*, TC 01:04:28

soap "The Truman Show" and its viewers and Truman's own perspective[147]. Consequently, the views about Truman's suburban world diverge extremely between the different audiences and also Truman himself at the beginning of the film. Unlike the viewers of the television show, the audience of the film is provided unfiltered insight into the studio work behind "The Truman Show", demonstrating that Truman is the producer's puppet and not a self-directed, individual being. When Truman is presented on screen to the theater audience for the first time, Weir employs a camera filming a television screen on which Truman is shown, which leads to a distortion concerning the vertical refresh rates. As a consequence, white vertical lines appear on the TV-screen and seemingly in front of Truman's face, which immediately evokes the impression in the spectators that they are watching a captive rather than a television star[148]. Therefore, as audience of the film, we immediately understand Truman's realm as dystopian, regarding Seahaven as nothing else but "a perverse and oppressive façade"[149].

For the television audience, Seahaven apparently evokes nostalgic images of the suburban space at the beginning of the film, as the set "seems to replicate a saccharine version of 1950s American suburbia"[150]. One does not learn a lot about the lives of the viewers of "The Truman Show", as they are only portrayed while watching the TV-show. With the exception of Sylvia, they are always presented from the perspective of their TV-sets, sometimes even looking right into the camera. Thus, the spectator of the film witnesses their longing gazes and their affections resulting from "The Truman Show", so their feelings towards the television series appear to be very similar to David's yearning towards the TV-show of "Pleasantville". For them, as one can see from their emotional and positive reactions to the show, the depicted suburban space of Seahaven marks a utopian enclave in an apparently dystopian society, giving them a bit of hope in a seemingly hopeless world – as Christof claims in the intro, many of the viewers leave "The Truman Show" on "all night, for comfort"[151]. This impression is underscored by the fact that the spectators are only shown in dark and closed interiors, which strongly contrasts to the colorful interiors of the houses in "The Truman Show" and also to the beautiful exterior shots of sunny Seahaven.

For Truman, too, Seahaven apparently marks a utopian, "comforting and idyllic home"[152] at the beginning of the film, as he owns a nice suburban house, is married to a beautiful young woman and surrounded by friendly neighbors and has a decent and respectable job as an

---

[147] Cf. Kammerer, Dietmar. *Bilder der Überwachung*. Frankfurt: Suhrkamp 2008, pp. 290-291
[148] See figures 3 and 4
[149] Marks 2005, p. 228
[150] Ibid.
[151] *The Truman Show*, TC 00:01:08
[152] Marks 2005, p. 228

insurance salesman. Indeed, thinking of the concept of the American Dream, he has everything that most people in America strive for. On first sight, he seems to be perfectly happy with his life, as he is smiling all the time and talks jokingly to his neighbors and colleagues when he is presented to the cinema audience at the beginning of the film. If one looks closer, however, one finds out that he simply adjusts to the general philosophy his environment imposes on him, which will be further discussed in the next paragraph. The falling spotlight therefore triggers the unmasking of Seahaven as a fully dystopian space for him.

It is interesting to note that at the beginning film, as Marks argues, "[t]hree levels of interpreters read the same space […] in markedly different ways"[153]. This shows once again how our expectations and experiences help to interpret and shape the suburban spaces which we perceive and in which me move. For the spectators of the TV-show, Seahaven marks a utopian space in the beginning because they *want* it to be a paradise, as watching Truman in the 1950s suburban neighborhood satisfies their nostalgic image of what life in suburbia should look like, in spite of knowing that this idealized view does not work in their reality. In contrast to the show, the film *The Truman Show* reveals itself as a postmodern text from the very beginning, leaving the audience no room to join the television audience in fantasizing about Seahaven as a paradise. As the film progresses, the initially different perspectives on Truman's world converge more and more to the conclusion that he is in fact a captive of a dystopian society from which he wants to escape.

6.3 The space of Seahaven: The utopian artifice of suburbia

At the beginning of the film, Weir uses a range of establishing shots to introduce the picturesque and pleasant 1950s-style suburban area of Seahaven to the spectators. Within the town, commercial spaces are conceptually separated from the dwelling areas, which is made visible by the fact that Truman takes the car to go to work although, given the small size of the town, he could easily walk there or go by bike. Again, like Pleasantville, Seahaven is a storybook-example of how spaces and life in a suburb should look like according to the postwar ideal. Truman's neighborhood is characterized by large and almost identical looking, Victorian-style single homes strung together in a very homogeneous way. The houses all come with a large front yard and white picket-fences, which makes Seahaven look very similar to Pleasantville. Whereas the latter is presented in black and white to the spectator for most of the time, the excessive use of colors on the houses in Truman's neighborhood makes

---

[153] Ibid.

34

the carefully designed town look even more appealing against the blue sky and sunlight. Large palm trees rustle gently in the wind in every front yard, and "outside" one can hear birds chirping. When Weir presents the suburb from above in an overview shot, one can see that Seahaven is an island, limited by the ocean on one side and by a large river on the other and seemingly surrounded by a huge forest[154]. Like in Pleasantville, nature and dwelling thus seem to match perfectly in Truman's hometown. In addition to the beautiful setting, life in general seems to be much more enjoyable and easier in Seahaven than in contemporary America on first sight. There is no hustle and bustle in the TV-show, as everyone has safe jobs, stable relationships and plenty of time for leisure activities or garden work. Watched from the outside, accordingly, "[the] world of Seahaven is an idealised one, the kind of romanticized idyllic life the past never was, but we all seem to desire to remember it as"[155].

While at the beginning of *Pleasantville*, Ross demonstrates that the inhabitants' lives are defined by habitual behavior and every day routines, Weir goes one step further in *The Truman Show* by demonstrating that the lives of the characters in the suburban space of Seahaven are characterized by endless repetitions: Except for Truman's family and acquaintances, all other people depicted on screen of "The Truman Show" are extras having their fixed first positions and prescribed range of actions. Thus, they are on a continual loop, moving without any purpose except for keeping Truman unaware of the artificiality of his life. Whereas Christof, the creator of the show, "believes completely in his own version of utopia"[156] and the privilege he has given to Truman, the latter is terribly bored by his meaningless existence and fantasizes about leaving Seahaven to see more of the world. As a result, the producer literally moves heaven and earth to "keep Truman in Seahaven and in the dark"[157] by missing no opportunity to point to the town's perfection: When Truman drives to work, the radio host joyfully proclaims "another beautiful day in paradise", the local newspaper's headline reads that Seahaven is the "Best Place on Earth" and even his "friend" Marlon tries to convince him that Seahaven is the only place to be:

TRUMAN
What was the furthest you ever got off the island?
MARLON
I went all over. Never found a place like this, though. Look at this sunset, Truman. It's   perfect.[158]

These attempts on Christof's side clearly demonstrate that the apparent utopia of Seahaven is in fact a dystopia in disguise, achieved by the consequent suppression of Truman's individual

---

[154] At the beginning of the film, the spectators do not know that Seahaven is a studio dome.
[155] http://www.virtualworldlets.net/Resources/Hosted/Resource.php?Name=TheTrumanShow
[156] Mercadante 2001, p. 3
[157] Ibid.
[158] *The Truman Show*, TC 00:34:55

desires. The more the creator of the show tries to convince Truman of the perfectness of Seahaven through various means, however, the more uneasy the latter gets about the very reality of his life, and the more synthetic and dystopian the depicted space appears to the spectator. This impression of artificiality is moreover highlighted by Weir's complex variation of camera shots: As Simone Knox points out, the director constantly changes between "film" cameras, portraying rather objective point-of-views only visible to the cinema audience, and "television" cameras, belonging to "The Truman Show" and filmed by the hidden cameras in the studio dome[159]. Especially the shots of the television cameras appear unusual and disconcerting to the theater audience, as Weir makes use of "stylistic devices ranging from the wide angle lens with vignetted edges"[160] to extreme camera angles, visible zooming and hasty movements, for instance when filmed from a camera that is attached to an actor or Truman himself. These camera techniques therefore create vertiginous feelings in the spectators which stand in strong opposition to the apparent stability and safety of life in Seahaven Christof wants to display to Truman. It is at all times obvious that Truman is followed by the cameras and controlled by the production team, so that the suburban space of Seahaven appears threatening and imprisoning to the audience despite its utopian surface.

6.4 Seahaven between simulacra and simulation

As Beuka puts it, suburbia is depicted as nothing more than "an artificial reconstruction of small-town America"[161] in *The Truman Show*. Seahaven is a giant simulacrum in which the creator of a television-show has fashioned a version of the idealized 1950s suburban space so elaborately that it *appears* real, although, following Baudrillard's definition of the simulacrum, "it has no relation to any reality whatsoever"[162]. Suburbia in *The Truman Show* is the nostalgic replication of a historical suburban space that never existed in reality, thus "nostalgia for a lost referential"[163]. Within the film, too, the question of reality is a very complex one: As Knox notes, *The Truman Show* demonstrates that the "distinctions between the real and the simulated have become problematic"[164]. Although the film seems to be about the opposition of real and simulation on first sight, a closer analysis of *The Truman Show* reveals that the lines between the two are constantly shown to be blurred. This ambivalence is already introduced at the very beginning of the film, when Christof asserts the sincerity of

---

[159] For a more detailed analysis on the complex interaction between different camera techniques, see Knox, Simone. "Reading *The Truman Show* Inside Out." *Film Criticism* 35, No. 1 (2010), pp. 3-4.
[160] Knox 2010, p. 4
[161] Beuka 2004, p. 227
[162] Baudrillard 2010, p. 6
[163] Ibid., p. 44
[164] Knox 2010, p. 2

"The Truman Show" to the spectator despite the fakeness of the depicted space, by claiming that "[although Truman's] world is, in some respects, counterfeit, there is nothing fake about Truman himself"[165].

In this context, the audience of the television show plays a crucial role too, as they also tend to confuse reality and fiction. When two waitresses are shown in the "Truman Bar" while they are watching the scene in which Truman remembers his lost love Silvia/Lauren, they seem to be fully aware of the artificiality of the show at first:

> **WAITRESS 1**
> What's he doing?
> **WAITRESS 2**
> See, they got rid of her, but they couldn't erase the memory.[166]

A couple of minutes later, however, after the insertion of a sample of flashbacks in "The Truman Show" depicting how Truman met Silvia, they seem to regard the action presented on screen as either completely fictional or completely true:

> **WAITRESS 1**
> Why didn't he just follow her to Fiji?
> **WAITRESS 2**
> His mother got sick, really sick. He couldn't leave her. He's kind – maybe he's too kind.[167]

In this situation, the two women are apparently not aware of the facts that on the one hand, Silvia is an actress that did not really go to Fiji but was simply expelled from the show, and that Truman could never follow her because he is forced to stay in the studio system in order to satisfy the viewers, who are an important part of the control system, too.[168]

The distinction between reality and simulation is moreover distorted on another level, which concerns the role of the television audience as a contrasting entity to the TV-show: Within the realm of the film, the viewers of "The Truman Show" are representatives of the *real*, contemporary America, whereas most of the action portrayed in the show is performed, or *simulated*. Nevertheless, the spectators of the show are also characterized by simulation: On the one hand, most of them appear in groups of two or three wearing identical clothes, therefore always being the doppelganger or replication of each other.[169] Apart from that, there are recurring items and patterns of "The Truman Show" found in the sequences in which the viewers are presented to the film audience, like for instance the typical check and floral fabrics Meryl often wears on screen or the huge colorful mugs Truman uses when drinking cocoa. As Christof tells the interviewer in the TV-special, all items in the show are for sale, to be ordered directly from the Truman catalogue. Therefore, while "The Truman Show"

---

[165] *The Truman Show*, TC 00:00:27
[166] Ibid., TC 00:18:21
[167] Ibid., TC 00:26:43
[168] See next paragraph.
[169] See figures 5-7

imitates reality, people of the "real" world aim to resemble their favorite characters in the show and therefore enter into the mode of simulation as well. One can clearly interpret this satirical portrayal of the viewers as Weir's criticism of the impact of the television and the advertising industry on people's individual spaces.

Coming back to the suburban space of Seahaven, one could conclude that it is a "gigantic simulacrum based on mythical American small-town life"[170], apparently meant to "[confirm] the extent to which [suburbia] has been, since the postwar years, very much an imagined environment, a landscape of the mind"[171], a nostalgic space without a referential. What is most ironic about Weir's film is that the suburban setting, which is supposed to seem real to Truman but in the film functions as a completely *fictional*, master-planned simulacrum, is in fact shot on a *real* location, being filmed in Seaside, Florida. Marks calls this selection of setting a "peculiar postmodern twist"[172], as it once again demonstrates that the opposition of reality and fiction collapses in the age of postmodernism, making it impossible to separate the one from the other. By employing the real town of Seaside as the physical space to portray the suburban simulacrum in *The Truman Show,* which "in turn was meant to mirror old-fashioned American suburbia"[173], Weir apparently makes a strong meta-textual, critical comment on the intertwining of nostalgic visions of suburbia and contemporary planned and gated communities.[174] Moreover, he adds yet another layer of simulation to the film, which creates a "mise-en-abyme"[175], or eternal mirror, concerning the question of drawing the line between fiction and reality, or *inside* and *outside*[176]. This is where "*The Truman Show* takes Baudrillard seriously"[177]:

> In America cinema is true because it is the whole of space, the whole way of life that are cinematic. The break between the two, the abstraction which we   deplore, does not exist: life is cinema.[178]

As Fitting notes, the film suggests that we live in a "reality culture", in which "new technologies have made it impossible to tell the real from the copy or the simulacrum"[179]. This demonstrates once more that suburbia, particularly because of the imposed "convergence

---

[170] Knox 2010, p. 2

[171] Beuka 2004, p. 229

[172] Marks 2005, p. 228

[173] Beuka 2004, p. 229

[174] See Beuka 2004, p. 229

[175] Following Susan Hayward's definition, a mise-en abyme is "a play of signifiers within a text, of sub-texts mirroring each other. This mirroring can get to a point where meaning can be rendered unstable and in this respect can be seen as a part of the process of deconstruction". See Hayward, Susan. *Cinema Studies: The Key Concepts.* New York: Routledge 2006, p. 222

[176] This echoes Derrida's famous dictum: "There's nothing outside the text".

[177] Wise, J. Macgregor. "Mapping the Culture of Control. Seing through *The Truman Show*". *Television and New Media 2002*; Vol. 3, No. 1, p. 35

[178] Baudrillard 1989, p. 101

[179] Fitting 2003, p. 158

of contemporary and postwar visions of suburbia"[180], is a highly ambivalent and complex space between reality and fiction according to *The Truman Show*.

6.5 "On the air. Unaware": Surveillance and control in *The Truman Show*

In dystopian societies, as Ferns argues, the citizens do not only have to obey to the standards set by the authorities, but "they must be *seen* to conform, and it is this visible conformity which is seen as essential to the preservation of stability"[181]. In Seahaven, which one can easily call a dystopian *state* due its political, hierarchical order of authorities, Truman is the only true citizen who is subject to "public scrutiny"[182], as all the other characters portrayed on screen are also part of the state's system. Already at the very beginning of *The Truman Show*, Weir makes it clear that surveillance and control are central characteristics defining both the space of Seahaven and "The Truman Show" in general: When the actor who plays Marlon gives an interview to the audience of the show, he wants to assure them of the authenticity of the actions depicted on screen in an interview by proclaiming that "[it's] all true, it's all real. Nothing here is fake. Nothing you see on the show is fake. It's merely *controlled*"[183].

In his essay "Mapping the Culture of Control", Wise notes that the two theories that are central to Weir's film are Michel Foucault's approach of the disciplinary society on the one hand, and Gilles Deleuze's theory of the control society on the other. Foucault's work on discipline results from his theories of organization and punishment in prisons. His central idea to bring order to "human multiplicities" [184], briefly speaking, is to employ various modern techniques, as for instance "timetables, collective training, exercises, total and detailed surveillance"[185]. His visions of the disciplinary society derive from his model of the Panopticon, a prison designed by Jeremy Bentham in the 18th century. As Wise notes, the "key to this model of disciplinarity was not the constant gaze, but the *potential* or threat of constant gaze"[186], as the prisoners never knew when they were observed and therefore had to watch and discipline themselves in order not to be punished. Therefore, according to his theory, the prisoner also begins to monitor the others as a result of the constant threat of being

---

[180] Beuka 2004, p. 229
[181] Ferns 1999, pp. 112-113; His emphasis.
[182] Ibid., p. 112
[183] *The Truman Show*, TC 00:00:50
[184] Foucault, Michel. "Panopticism". In: Rabinow, Paul (Ed.). *The Foucault Reader*. New York: Pantheon Books 1984, p. 207
[185] Ibid., p. 209
[186] Wise 2002, p. 30; Emphasis added.

surveilled: In the disciplinary society, "not only do we self-discipline but we discipline each other"[187].

Gilles Deleuze argues, however, that Foucault's theories are only applicable to "spaces of enclosure"[188] (e.g. prisons, hospitals, schools), the borders of which in contemporary culture are dissolving gradually[189]. In Deleuze's opinion, society has undergone a transition from discipline to control: "We're moving toward control societies that no longer operate by confining people but through continuous control and instant communication"[190]. His central metaphor in this respect is the highway, as "a highway does not confine one, but it does control one's movements, the options available to one"[191]. Control, in other words, has become undetectable, as it is precisely the individual's ability to move within open spaces that the control society makes use of.[192] Although there is no confinement anymore, the individual has to follow the rules of the society at any given time, as in contrast to disciplinary techniques that start over at each space of enclosure, measures of control are invisible and ever changing, always adjusting to the respective situation:

> Enclosures are *molds*, distinct castings, but controls are *modulations*, like a self-deforming cast that will continuously change from one moment to the other, or like a sieve whose mesh will transmute from point to point.[193]

As has been stated already in the preceding chapters, 5,000 cameras are installed in the studio dome of Seahaven filming every single movement and emotional reaction of Truman to be broadcasted live in all countries of the world, which echoes Foucault's model of the Panopticon to a large extent. Truman's environment is in fact an enclosed space, guarded and monitored by the producer, the TV-crew and in a way also by the audience of the show. Moreover, in order to keep him inside the realm of the TV-series, the society of Seahaven has disciplined Truman again and again, particularly traumatizing him with water. Nevertheless, "The Truman Show" portrays a society of control rather than of discipline, mostly because Foucault's Panopticism only works because of the individuals' constant threat of being watched. Truman, however, has been completely *unaware* of the television cameras for the first thirty years of his life.

As Wise notes, the key to the understanding of "The Truman Show" is continuous modulation[194], as every misdirected movement on Truman's side is countered by members of

---

[187] Wise 2002, p. 30
[188] Deleuze, Gilles. "Postscript on the Societies of Control". *October.* Vol. 59. (Winter, 1992), p. 3
[189] Cf. Wise 2002, p. 31; Kammerer 2008, p. 131
[190] Deleuze, Gilles. *Negotiations.* Columbia University Press: New York 1990, p. 176
[191] Wise 2002, p. 31
[192] Cf. Kammerer 2008, pp. 133-34
[193] Deleuze 1992, p. 4
[194] Cf. Wise 2002, p. 36

the cast obeying to the instructions of Christof. Therefore, although Truman believes to be able to move freely and independently at first, in fact his whole life has been controlled and managed by the crew of the TV-show. In this context, the control system proves to be much more successful than that of discipline: As soon as Truman finds out that he is restricted by the others, he instantly starts to revolt against the newly discovered society of discipline.

6.6 Truman's escape from dystopia: hope for suburbia?

After Truman has finally left the giant studio dome, we are presented different groups of the TV-audience applauding and rejoicing at his escape from Seahaven. Obviously, they have changed their minds of the depicted suburban space in the course of the last episodes of "The Truman Show", also considering it as dystopian in the end. However, what seems like a perfect happy ending on first sight leaves a sour taste on a closer look. On the one hand, the end of the film does not really focus on Truman's liberation, but on the viewers' reactions to it. The last shot presents two watchmen, ironically, who neither watch their monitors nor the parking lots but instead stare into the TV-set in which they only see the static noise[195]. When the one asks the other "What else is on?", it becomes clear that they are still "trapped in the dystopian world of reality television viewing"[196] and that the seemingly positive ending of "The Truman Show" is pointless as it does not change their perception of their own world of control. On the other hand, the question arises whether Truman's escape really results in a better life for him. As Dietmar Kammerer notes, Truman may have left the panoptic, disciplinary society of the studio dome at the end of the film, but outside of it he is still trapped in Deleuze's society of control[197]. As Beuka notes in his essay "The View through the Picture Window", the film's "emphasis [...] on control and imprisonment as old-time community" reminds the spectator of the thinking behind the popular gated communities, a fact that "lends added weight to [Truman's] entrapment and eventual escape, as well as the viewer's voyeuristic involvement in both"[198].

Concerning everyday suburban life, the film offers an even more sinister insight. As Halper and Muzzio argue, although *The Truman Show* addresses multiple topics, such as television, voyeurism, consumerism and certainly surveillance and control, its main point

---

[195] Cf. Kammerer 2008, p. 291; See *The Truman Show*, 01:32:00
[196] Marks 2005, p. 228
[197] Cf. Kammerer 2008, p. 292
[198] Beuka, Robert. "The View through the Picture Window: Surveillance and Entrapment Motifs in Suburban Film". In: Blauvelt, Andrew (Ed.). *Worlds Away. New Suburban Landscapes*. Walker Art Center: Minneapolis 2008, p. 99

seems to be about suburbia.[199] Like *Pleasantville*, Weir's film mirrors the fictionality of the postwar ideal of suburban existence, which brings us back to the initial problem of the authenticity of 1950s suburbia, the period which is in a way fabricated and therefore conserved in "The Truman Show". As Lynn Spigel points out in her essay "From theatre to space ship – metaphors of suburban domesticity in postwar America", already in the 1950s "domestic life [was] a kind of stage", and suburbia characterized by the "theatrical quality of everyday life"[200]. As she notes,

> [home] manuals, magazines, and advertisements extended this emphasis on the home as a showcase, recommending ways to create glamorous backgrounds on which to enact spectacular scenes.[201]

Thus, Weir seems to make evident particularly this theatricality of suburban life with his film, as he shows how the domestic space – not only within the show, but also in contemporary America – is shaped by advertisements and consumer goods rather than interpersonal relationships. In Halper and Muzzio's words: "If our ideal living place can be purposely built for television, how shallow must it be – and if we love and consider it home, how shallow must *we* be!"[202]

---

[199] Halper and Muzzio 2002, p. 550
[200] Spigel, Lynn. "From Theatre to Space Ship. Metaphors of Suburban Domesticity in Postwar America". In: Silverstone, Roger (Ed.). *Visions of Suburbia*. London and New York: Routledge 1997, p. 220
[201] Ibid., p. 221
[202] Halper and Muzzio 2002, p. 550; Emphasis added.

7. "Look Closer": Suburbia as imprisoning dystopia in *American Beauty*

7.1 Introduction and plot summary

In *American Beauty*, published in 1999, Sam Mendes depicts the contemporary American suburbs as spaces of conformity, dysfunction and repression. The film focuses on the last months of 42-year-old marketing magazine writer Lester Burnham who lives in a random suburban neighborhood together with his wife Carolyn, who is a rather unsuccessful real estate agent, and their teenage daughter Jane. Due to his monotonous job in the advertising branch, his shattered marriage and alienated family life, the writer is terribly bored and frustrated by his existence. When he meets Jane's best friend Angela for the first time, he immediately feels attracted to her, and capturing her attention becomes his new sense of life. In addition, he feels inspired by his neighbors' son Ricky Fitts, who pretends to earn money with catering jobs but instead successfully deals with drugs. Taking the young man as his personal idol, Lester quits his job to work in a fast food restaurant, starts working out to impress Angela and, with the help of Ricky as his dealer, starts smoking Marihuana. By revolting against his societal obligations as the breadwinning head of the family, he also turns the lives of the other protagonists upside down: Carolyn starts an affair with one of her real estate competitors and Jane falls in love and plans her escape from suburbia with Ricky. Due to some misunderstandings, Ricky's father, a retired US Marine Corps colonel, believes his son to be a callboy having sex with Lester for money. When he visits Lester in the latter's garage, the colonel tries to kiss the writer on the mouth in an act of confusion. Because Lester refuses his homosexual advances, Mr. Fitts walks out without saying a word. In the same night, Carolyn is left by her lover after Lester has found out about them. As a result, because she blames him for her miserable life, she drives home to kill Lester with a handgun. Meanwhile, when Lester returns into the house after the incident with the colonel, he meets Angela in the living room as she stays the night over at the Burnhams' house. They are just about to sleep with each other when she tells him that she is a virgin. As a result, he decides not to sleep with her, and from that time onwards acts like a father figure. Just when Lester has apparently found his true self again, Colonel Fitts enters the kitchen from behind and shoots the former into the head.

7.2 Utopia or dystopia? The introduction of the suburban space of *American Beauty*

Although in contrast to *Pleasantville* and *The Truman Show*, Mendes employs contemporary American suburbia as the setting of his story, the suburban neighborhood presented in

American Beauty shares a lot of visual elements with the replicated and idealized versions of postwar suburbs depicted in the other two films. Like the Parkers (*Pleasantville*) and the Burbanks (*The Truman Show*), the Burnhams own a huge single home with a large and well-kept front yard, framed by the typical white picket fence like all the other houses in the street. As the Burnhams' house is painted in white, red and blue, it reminds the spectator of the American flag, a presentation that ties the suburban space seen in the film closely to the USA. The yard contains carefully set bushes of red roses like in *Pleasantville*, stressing the importance of green and natural spaces in the suburb. As a result, everything about the suburban landscape depicted in the film looks pleasant and beautiful on the surface.

As I have argued in the third chapter, "[every] utopia always comes with its implied dystopia"[203] and vice versa. In *American Beauty*, one perceives a neatly designed, Edenic suburban space in which seemingly perfect families live their American Dreams. On a closer look, however, one finds out that the characters merely keep up an image of being successful and happy, while their lives are marked by repression, frustrations and estrangement in fact. This becomes obvious from the beginning of *American Beauty* onwards, as the utopian visual aesthetics is played against by Lester's Noir-esque[204] posthumous voice-over-narration:

> **LESTER (VO)**
> My name is Lester Burnham. This is my neighborhood. This is my street. This... is my life. I'm forty-two years old. In less than a year, I'll be dead. [...]
> Of course, I don't know that yet. And in a way... I'm dead already.[205]

When Mendes introduces Lester's random suburban neighborhood to the spectators in the beginning, he makes use of a panoramic shot, depicting "a bland and uniform streetscape [...] merging into an amorphous blob of picket-fenced domesticity"[206]. Sikivu Hutchinson notes that already this opening aerial shot, together with the cynical voice-over narration, works as a "seductive device for introducing the film's narrative of dysfunctionality [and] a mediation on the premature death of the suburban ideal"[207]. This shot is repeated several times at "key turning points of the narrative and again at the end of the film"[208], mapping the tragedy of the film clearly to the suburban landscape.

---

[203] Gordin, Tilley and Prakash 2010, p. 2; See also Chapter 3
[204] In the American Film Noir cycle (approx. 1942-1958), the employment of male voice-over narration was regularly used to convey the impression of hopelessness and tragic fate.
[205] http://www.dailyscript.com/scripts/AmericanBeauty_final.html; See *American Beauty*, TC 00:01:14
[206] Law, Shirley. "Looking Closer: Structure, Style and Narrative in *American Beauty*". *Screen Education*, No. 43 (2006), p. 125
[207] Hutchinson, Sikivu. ""Look Closer": The White Spaces of American Beauty". In: *Spectator: The University of Southern California Journal of Film and Television Critics*, Vol.21.1. (Spring 2001), p. 37
[208] Beuka 2008, p. 99

As the film continues, it makes us "peer voyeuristically"[209] into the Burnham's home and marriage, which, according to Lester, is a "commercial for how normal [they] are when [they] are anything but"[210]. The nuclear family, which according to the postwar ideal forms the most basic unit of suburbia, is thus presented as a hollow image veiling the alienation between the family members. Mendes moreover alludes to the artificiality involved in the everyday lives of the Burnham family when he introduces Lester's wife to the spectator. The camera first cuts to a close-up of a bright red rose, which is clipped by Carolyn, who then thoroughly investigates it in terms of perfection. Continuing his voice-over-narration, Lester tells the spectator that her matching gardening clocks and shears are no coincidence, which already indicates that she is obsessed with outer appearances. In this scene, the director already introduces the 'American Beauty' rose as a leitmotif of the film, apparently functioning as a metaphor for surface beauty reminding the spectator of the fact that "there must be a worm somewhere"[211]. When Jim makes her a compliment about her roses, she admits that keeping them beautiful involves a lot of care:

JIM
I just love your roses. How do you get them to flourish like this?
CAROLYN
Well, I'll tell you. Egg shells and 'Miracle Grow'.[212]

This conversation makes it clear to the spectator that the roses are not perfect by nature as it requires a lot of (chemical) care from outside to make them *look* beautiful. If one interprets the rose as a symbol of her family life in this situation, Carolyn therefore subliminally admits that it takes a lot of work in order to keep up the *image* of a perfect suburban family against the rottenness lying within. As Halper and Muzzio point out, "[suburbia] in *American Beauty* represents the highest stage of bourgeois inauthenticity"[213], because what seems like the realization of the utopian, idealized suburban existence for the depicted characters turns out to be a dystopian world of imprisonment, conformity and "overpowering materialism"[214] for most of the movie.

---

[209] Ibid.

[210] *American Beauty*, TC 01:36:16

[211] Hewison, David. "Oh Rose, thou art sick! Anti-individuation Forces in the Film *American Beauty*". *Journal of Analytical Psychology*, Vol. 48, No. 5. (Nov. 2003), p. 691. In fact, the American Beauty rose is susceptible to a variety of diseases and pests, often already rotting on the inside while still looking perfect on the outside, see http://backyardgardener.com/plantname/pda_fb10.html.

[212] http://www.dailyscript.com/scripts/AmericanBeauty_final.html; See *American Beauty*, TC 00:02:46

[213] Halper and Muzzio 2002, p. 550

[214] Spector, Judith; Tsiopos Willis, Katherine. "The Aesthetics of Materialism in Alan Ball's *American Beauty*." *Midwest Quarterly*. 48, no. 2 (2007), p. 279

7.3 Defining the dystopia of *American Beauty*: Suburbia as a prison

As David Smith notes in his essay "'Beautiful Necessities:' *American Beauty* and the Idea of Freedom", with regard to suburbia, Mendes conveys the message that "life tends to go stale within the confines of a picket-fence, consumerist, career-driven version of the American dream"[215]. Especially with regard to Lester, the director puts a lot of effort into showing that the writer is completely frustrated by and stuck in his suburban routines and boredom. In this context, the impression of Lester's imprisonment is underscored most obviously by means of cinematic techniques and carefully chosen settings. Particularly at the very beginning of the film, Mendes portrays the protagonist in various kinds of visual "jail cells", as the director states in the simultaneous commentary track on the DVD-version of *American Beauty*, as Lester is mostly shown in narrow and closed interiors and visually confined by the framing of the respective shots.

In one of the first scenes in which Lester is presented on screen, he is shown standing under the shower being masturbating, which marks the "high point" of his day according to his voice-over narration. As the camera is located in front of the shower, it depicts Lester standing behind the foggy glass, with his body confined by the frames of the shower stall[216]. This mise-en-scène can be interpreted as an indication that sexual needs do not have a place in conservative American suburbia, and also signals that Lester and Carolyn do not share any physical relationship anymore. The feeling of confinement is moreover demonstrated when the protagonist is shown in the living room watching his wife tendering her roses in the front yard. Especially the scene in which Carolyn talks to Jim about her roses is decisive in this respect: The camera is located in Jim's garden, right in front of him and Carolyn who are talking to each other at the picket-fence. Lester, who is standing at the window of the living room, is presented in the middle of them, thus framed by his wife, his neighbor and the window screen at the same time, which links his confinement closely to both his marriage and the suburban landscape[217].

The motif of entrapment is further extended to Lester's work place, as the first time he is presented to the spectators at his office, his face is shown in a reflection on his computer screen. Because there are various vertical columns on the display, Lester once again looks like a prisoner behind bars[218]. Moreover, when the camera cuts to the grey and indefinite open-plan office, the spectators realize that Lester is in fact sitting in an office cube between

---

[215] Smith, David. "'Beautiful Necessities': *American Beauty* and the Idea of Freedom". *Journal of Religion and Film*, Vol. 6, No. 2 (October 2002), pp. 1-2
[216] See figure 8
[217] See figure 9
[218] See figure 10

numerous others, which demonstrates his insignificance once again. This impression is even strengthened when he talks to his boss in the latter's office, as Mendes films Lester from a great distance and from high angle positions, making him look isolated and inferior to his much younger boss.

Although unlike Truman, Lester does not literally live in an enclosed space, he is still trapped in his suburban life by means of everyday routines and the expectations of his wife, his boss and society in general at the beginning of the movie. The dystopian world of *American Beauty* is thus not an authoritarian state like in *The Truman Show*, but apparently created by the imposition of the stereotypical, suburban ideal and the subsequent neglect of individual desires to save this ideal. As a consequence, Lester is "[caught] in a web of obligations, hatred and self-hatred"[219] at the beginning of the film, which is underscored by the fact that he is depicted being visually confined on screen almost without exception. Metaphorically speaking, the obligations imposed on Lester therefore extremely delimit his individual space.

Typically for a protagonist in a dystopian narrative, Lester becomes more and more alienated by his environment and starts to question the rigid and oppressive structures keeping him in his role-play. Therefore, he "rebels against the world of appearances"[220] which becomes obvious for the first time when Carolyn tries to convince Lester to subordinate to his boss in order to keep his job:

> **CAROLYN**
> --there is no decision, you just write the damn thing!
> **LESTER**
> You don't think it's weird and kinda fascist?
> **CAROLYN**
> Possibly. But you don't want to be unemployed.
> **LESTER**
> Oh, well, let's just all sell our souls and work for Satan, because it's more convenient that way. [221]

The turning point concerning Lester's breaking out of his suburban routines is initiated not only by his first sight of his sexual object Angela, but also by his first encounter with Ricky Fitts at Carolyn's business dinner. When Ricky's boss finds the two of them smoking dope on the roof and wants Ricky to get back to his word as a bartender, the teenager simply quits his job and thus becomes Lester's "personal hero", as the young man does not stick to the rules of society. When the writer leaves the roof to follow Carolyn, Mendes uses an extreme long shot to show the huge distance between Ricky's liberal way of life and Lester's boredom and frustration. The camera then portrays Lester standing inside the door, while he is again

---

[219] Halper and Muzzio 2002, p. 550
[220] Beuka 2008, p. 99
[221] http://www.dailyscript.com/scripts/AmericanBeauty_final.html; See *American Beauty*, TC 00:05:59

visually confined not only by the frame, but also by the vertical blinds behind him. When Lester closes the door behind him and leaves Ricky standing on the roof, one can read the scene as Lester's return into his old life, separating himself from Ricky's world of freedom and self-determination for a last time.

7.4 The destructiveness of the American Dream in suburbia

As has already been pointed out at the beginning of this book, the suburban lifestyle became closely tied to the American Dream in the postwar period, which is why Amy Kenyon even calls suburbia the "spatialization of the American Dream" in *Dreaming Suburbia*[222]. In Mendes's film, the spectators are brought to the suburban "heartland of the American Dream, [...] home to a comfortable, prosperous, self-contented community"[223] on the one hand, but also a space "where discontent, lies and nightmares stir beneath the soft velvety appearance"[224], as David Hewison puts it. Compared to *Pleasantville* and *The Truman Show*, Mendes's film illustrates the interlacing of the suburban landscape and the Dream most obviously, as it shows how the portrayed citizens of suburbia are obsessed with keeping up the image of living their own American Dream while repressing their individual desires. As Kim Goudreau notes, the "suburban backdrop is an integral part of the film as the "stage" of the American dream"[225], hinting at the very theatricality of the characters' lives.

Without going too much into detail concerning the elusive concept of the American Dream[226], according to Caldwell, "it is an idealized notion of progress that lies in the heart of [it]"[227]. It has always "tended to divide itself into two distinct parts: the idealistic dream and the materialistic dream"[228], marking stories of ongoing development, hard work resulting in being both successful and happy and of coming closer to one's ideal life. At the beginning of *American Beauty*, as pointed out above, there is no progress in Lester's life at all, as he is depressed, frustrated, emotionless and "dead already", as he states in the voice-over narration. His seemingly perfect life is a dystopian prison in disguise from which he yearns to break out. Lester's life gets totally out of control after the encounter with Ricky, as the writer quits his well-paid job to work at a fast food restaurant, exercises in the garage like a maniac, starts

---

[222] Kenyon 2004, p. 1; See also Chapter 2.2
[223] Hewison 2003, p. 690
[224] Ibid.
[225] Goudreau, Kim. "*American Beauty*: The Seduction of the Visual Image in the Culture of Technology". *Bulletin of Science, Technology & Society* . Vol. 26.1 (2006), p. 23
[226] For a detailed analysis of the concept of the American Dream, see e.g. Freese, Peter. *The American Dream and the American Nightmare*. Paderborn: Paderborner Universitätsreden 1987; Caldwell, Wilber. *Cynicism and the Evolution of the American Dream*. Washington, D.C.: Potomac Books, Inc. 2006.
[227] Caldwell, 2006, p. 41
[228] Ibid., p. 39

drinking and smoking marihuana on a regular basis and sells his Toyota to buy a Pontiac Firebird. One could even say that his economical downfall represents a counter-movement to the notion of the American Dream.

As Halper and Muzzio argue, Lester experiences a "(nostalgic) awakening" as he tries to escape the "blandness of present suburban life [to reach for] a better suburbia"[229], a more genuine, open space in which he can do whatever he pleases. As a result of this change of mind, Lester transforms completely in terms of self-confidence and emotionality, apparently feeling authentic for the first time in years. While his self-motivated liberation of societal pressures and his suburban role as the breadwinning head of the family leads to an extreme emotional relief for him, he "acts as the internal trigger, destabilizing the social group"[230] of all the characters of *American Beauty*: With his desire-driven behavior, he shakes the grounds of the static suburban space of his neighborhood in a similar way David and Jennifer do in *Pleasantville*, as he threatens the seemingly perfect lives of the people around him, most of all that of his wife and the Colonel. Carolyn would not be able to maintain her image of a successful realtor with a drug-consuming husband or even a costly divorce. As Spector and Wills put it, "[her] dominant philosophy represents the American Dream poisoned by the worst aspects of consumerism"[231]. Frank Fitts's life would also fall apart if Lester told anyone about the former's repressed homosexuality. Because they are more afraid of their material and societal than of their moral downfall, both of them would rather kill Lester than risking their ideal world to collapse, which again displays the destructiveness of the American Dream and the suburban ideal of the nuclear family.

7.5 The suburbs as "picture windows": Voyeurism and control in suburbia

As Robert Beuka points out in *SuburbiaNation*,

> [the] recurring motif [of surveillance in suburban films] reflects a cultural perception of the suburb as a place where the distinctions between public and private lives have become blurred, a "picture window" world of visibility and compromised privacy.[232]

In *American Beauty*, too, surveillance and control are portrayed to be a significant factor of suburban existence. But whereas Truman is watched and controlled by the members of the authoritarian, dystopian state in *The Truman Show*, in Mendes's film, it is the citizens themselves who monitor each other. They make sure that everyone follows the unspoken but evident code of conduct of suburbia, namely that all neighbors are part of the community

---

[229] Halper and Muzzio 2002, p. 221
[230] Law 2006, p. 124
[231] Spector and Tsiopos Wills 2007, p. 281
[232] Beuka 2004, p. 237

without invading each other's private space. To illustrate this, the director employs a lot of scenes in which the characters of the film are watching their neighbors from a distance or through windows. In this context, the characters' urge for spatial detachment between houses is presented on screen for instance when Lester blames Carolyn for cutting their former neighbors' tree:

> **LESTER**
> Well, they were still mad at you for cutting down their sycamore.
> **CAROLYN**
> *Their* sycamore? C'mon! A substantial portion of the root structure was on our property. You know that. How can you call it their sycamore? I wouldn't have the heart to just cut down something if it wasn't partially mine, which of course it was.[233]

This conversation shows that Carolyn regards the picket-fence as a clear-cut border between her space and that of the neighbors, and that everyone who crosses this border must be disciplined immediately. By cutting her neighbors' tree, she has therefore redefined the limits of her property and underscored the significance of respecting each other's own private space in suburbia. As Amy Kenyon points out, the components of the suburban dream are "space, tamed greenery and a sense of community", characterized by the people's need for "safety and isolation [and] fear of individualism and controversy"[234]. This idea is picked up on when Carolyn attacks Jane for treating her mother disrespectfully:

> **CAROLYN**
> You ungrateful little brat. Just look at everything you have. When I was your age, I lived in a *duplex*! We didn't even have our own house.[235]

In this scene, one can see once again that for Carolyn, owning a single home which is detached from those of one's neighbors is one of the most important achievements in life. The community of the Burnhams' neighborhood is thus defined by very superficial bonds, as the characters try hard to keep their public lives distinct from their private ones, thus keeping the suburban space *static*. The scene also displays a kind of domestic discipline, which is found in a more extreme version in the Fitts' household, as the colonel does not only force his son to hand in urine samples on a regular basis, but also beats him up when he does not follow his father's rules. As Marcel O'Gorman notes, "parental discipline shields the privacy of the home (and thus of the children) from external influences by controlling the layout of domestic space as well as the objects within that space"[236].

However, in *American Beauty* the spectators learn that the separation of public and private spaces is impossible in contemporary suburbia, particularly in the light of modern technology.

---

[233] http://www.dailyscript.com/scripts/AmericanBeauty_final.html; See *American Beauty*, TC 00:06:20
[234] Kenyon 2004, p. 45
[235] *American Beauty*, TC 01:05:51
[236] O'Gorman, Marcel. "*American Beauty* Busted: Necromedia and Domestic Discipline". *SubStance*, Vol. 33, No. 3, Issue 105: Special Issue: Overload (2004), p. 42

Beuka argues, "[a]s in *The Truman Show*, once again we see surveillance and voyeurism as key to the depiction of a fractured suburban community"[237], which is represented in Mendes's film by the character of Ricky Fitts who regularly intrudes into his neighbors' private spaces by filming them with his video camera. By his "gaze through the picture window"[238], especially with the help of the camera zoom, he destroys the intimacy of suburban domesticity and makes the cleft between staged, public image and reality visible on his screen. In this respect, it is important to note that Ricky *records* his observations, which makes it possible for him (and others, as we see in the course of the movie) to watch the scenes over and over again. In terms of the other characters' urge to keep their private and public lives apart, Ricky ultimately violates the suburban conduct with his "electronically mediated intrusion of public space into the private domain"[239]. As a consequence, the private spaces of the characters are *inverted* as they become public on Ricky's screen. As O'Gorman argues, this new dynamics of space "can only be catastrophic for the domestic scene"[240]: Utterly confused by the homosexual drives resulting from his misunderstandings regarding Lester's depiction on Rickey's videos, the Colonel finally shoots the object of his non-conform desire, apparently both to protect Ricky and to restore his image as heterosexual head of the suburban family: "Never underestimate the power of denial", as Ricky states in an earlier scene, is therefore shown to be one of the essential messages concerning the representation of suburbia in *American Beauty*.

7.6 Hope for suburbia? The search for the true beauty in dystopia

From the title and throughout Mendes's film it is obvious that "[the] object of everyone's desire is beauty"[241]: Lester is seduced by Angela's youth and beautiful body; Carolyn is obsessed with her stunning roses and expensive furniture; Angela wants to be a famous model; even Jane strives for beauty, as she saves all her money from her babysitting jobs for a breast augmentation. As Spector and Wills argue, all the characters fall into the trap of confusing "'what we see' and 'what we want'", as they are blinded by the surface beauty of their different objects of desire[242]. Their central attitude of life is summed up by a statement Angela makes to Jane at some point of the film: "There's nothing worse in life than being

---

[237] Beuka 2008, p. 99
[238] Ibid.
[239] O'Gorman 2004, p. 45
[240] Ibid.
[241] Spector and Tsiopos Wills 2007, p. 281
[242] Ibid., p. 282

ordinary". It is precisely in this context that *American Beauty* invites the spectators to "Look Closer", which is the tagline and main principle of the movie.

Sam Mendes particularly uses Ricky's camera to unveil the artificiality of surface beauty: Although Ricky's spying and filming wreak havoc on the film's tragic plot, in an "ironic contemporary twist"[243], it also constitutes an effective stylistic technique to visualize the significance of looking closer. Positively speaking, he is the only character in the film attempting to look behind the curtains, both literally when he zooms through the picture windows of the Burnhams' house and figuratively when he focuses on people's faces to expose their emotions. With the help of his camera, he moreover captures the little details and banalities of life which would normally remain hidden from his eyes and also from those of the spectators of *American Beauty*. In this way, he enriches the otherwise static suburban space by rendering it both more fragile and more authentic, which echoes the coloring and expansion of space in *Pleasantville*[244].

Regarding the search for beauty as the leitmotif of *American Beauty*, the scene in which Ricky shows Jane his video of an empty plastic bag wafting through the air in a backyard of his suburban neighborhood certainly marks the key to the understanding of true beauty as portrayed in the film. Ricky calls it the most beautiful thing he has ever filmed, and enters into a monologue of beauty in general:

> **RICKY**
> […] That's the day I realized that there was this entire life behind things, and this incredibly benevolent force that wanted me to know there was no reason to be afraid. Ever. […]Sometimes there's so much beauty in the world I feel like I can't take it... and my heart is going to cave in.[245]

While Ricky is talking, the director alternately portrays scenes from the video and Jane's and Ricky's faces in extreme close-ups, which links their true emotional reactions closely to the action depicted on the TV-screen and makes the scene one of the most touching ones of the whole film. Mendes's choice of the plastic bag as an icon of true beauty is certainly no coincidence, as it stands for consumerism on the one hand, which is often criticized to be one of the central flaws of American suburbia, and on the other marks one of the most ordinary and meaningless items of everyday life. In this way, the bag stands in strong opposition to the recurring images of the American Beauty rose, which is vivid and beautiful on the surface but often rotten below its petals. With the help of this scene, Mendes seems to point out that the beauty and joy of life lie in the little details one often overlooks. Thus, the director again criticizes the way people struggle for perfection and success without accepting themselves as imperfect beings living in a dynamic and complex space.

---

[243] Beuka 2008, p. 99

[244] See Chapter 4.

[245] *American Beauty*, TC 01:00:26 – TC 01:01:32

Mendes takes up this idea once again at the end of the film through Lester's final monologue, when the latter talks about all the little things which made his life worth living, like "lying on [his] back on boy scouts camp, watching falling stars", or "the yellow leaves from the maple trees, that lined [his] street". Mendes moreover repeats the aerial shot that appears at several points of the movie. This time, however, the camera zooms *out*, making the spectator see a large part of the suburban landscape surrounding Lester's neighborhood when he says in his voice-over narration that he "cannot feel anything but gratitude for every single moment of [his] stupid little life". Like in *Pleasantville*, the closing of *American Beauty* thus finally embraces the space of contemporary suburbia, as it reveals that real beauty is found even "in so depressing, dysfunctional, and imprisoning an environment as the suburb"[246].

---

[246] Beuka 2008, p. 99

8. Conclusion and outlook

As I have pointed out throughout this book, the depiction of suburbia in contemporary American cinema portrays the suburban landscape as a highly ambiguous cultural space which is never neutral, but rather constantly moving between dystopian and utopian presentations. In all the films discussed, at the very moment the utopian ideal is unveiled as an imagined one, the dystopia of suburbia is exposed and works as an explanation for the protagonists' downfalls. While *Pleasantville* and *The Truman Show* allegorically and didactically investigate the static and seemingly safe postwar ideal of American suburbia by challenging its very authenticity and by opposing it to visions of present-day American suburbia, *American Beauty* focuses on the dystopian, dysfunctional aspects of the contemporary suburbs, which, according to the film, result from the overpowering influence of materialism and conformity and the misinterpretation of the American Dream. Even if the films still tend to alternate between utopian and dystopian aspects of suburbia, this book has shown that there is a progress from the strong oppositions between the imagined and the contemporary space of suburbia, as depicted in *Pleasantville,* to a more opened-up and authentic representation as found in *American Beauty.* Although they do not find a true resolution for the tensions found in the suburban space, as all of them are "unable to imagine an economic alternative within a believable quotidian framework"[247], the films still convey a feeling of hope for the suburban existence in the closing scenes and a tendency to appreciate contemporary suburbia in spite of and even *because* of its complexity.

In the light of the postmodern approaches of Baudrillard and Jameson as cited earlier in this book, any strong opposition between utopia and dystopia to describe the suburban space is naturally doomed to failure, simply because in their opinion, binaries are about to collapse into one another and cannot exist in our culture anymore[248]. In this context, although the three films are still caught between images of the two-sidedness of suburban existence, their ambivalent endings, especially that of *American Beauty*, indicate a trend for overcoming these oppositions, as all of them finally embrace present-day suburbia as a rich and highly dynamic space.

A number of critics argue in a similar way by challenging a "reductive, two-dimensional vision of suburbia"[249]. New York Times columnist David Brooks, for instance, claims that

---

[247] Gournelos, Ted. "Othering the Self: Dissonant Visual Culture and Quotidian Trauma in United States Suburbia". *Cultural Studies <=> Critical Methodologies.* vol. 9, no. 4. August 2009, p. 519
[248] See Chapters 2 and 4
[249] Beuka 2004, p. 4

suburbia is just "the latest iteration of the American dream"[250], as people living in the suburbs today are still motivated in the same way by the myth of progress the first generation of American citizens was hundreds of years ago. For him, the suburban *imagination*, or "mysterious longing"[251], critics often disapprove is the exact essence that defines the American culture. Although he admits that suburbia is marked by consumerism and conformity, being the landscape of "Slurp&Gulps, McDonald's, Disney, breast enlargements and 'The Bachelor'", he claims that there is nevertheless "an imaginative fire that animates Americans and [that] propels [them] to work hard, move so much and leap so wantonly"[252]. In his whole article, he therefore conveys the message that it is precisely the tension between suburbia as an *imagined* space and the problems found in the *real* space of contemporary suburbs that creates the dynamics which characterizes the American spirit in general. Consequently, one can conclude that the complex contemporary suburban space essentially mirrors the American mentality as a whole.

Following Beuka's final conclusion, the treatment of suburbia in *American Beauty* summarizes the fictional works on the suburban landscape at the turn of the century, as it shows that "the suburban question has become increasingly complex"[253]. Thus, the films do not offer a true resolution precisely because there is none: We have to accept both the idealized images of the suburban space and the dangers and merits involved in suburban dwelling as parts of the same package. Despite the tensions resulting from the ever-surviving postwar suburban ideal on the one side and the social problems and tensions that are mapped to contemporary suburbia on the other, the suburban landscape for Americans is not a *no-place*, neither hell nor Paradise, but "the most profound and vexing of all environments: home"[254].

---

[250] Brooks, David. "Our Sprawling, Supersize Utopia". *New York Times Magazine*; Apr 4, 2004; New York Time, p. 46
[251] Ibid.
[252] Ibid.
[253] Ibid., p. 243
[254] Ibid.

List of figures

Figure 1: A Westec patrol driving through contemporary suburbia

Figure 2: The geography of Pleasantville

Figure 3: Truman as a captive behind visual prison bars (© Paramount
1999 – All rights reserved)

Figure 4: Filming the screen: Several layers of mediation (© Paramount
1999 – All rights reserved)

Figure 5: Doppelgangers as symbols of simulation and simulacra
(© Paramount 1999 – All rights reserved)

Figure 6: Doppelgangers wearing Meryl's bathrobe (© Paramount 1999 – All rights reserved)

Figure 7: Doppelgangers in the 'Truman Bar' (© Paramount 1999 – All rights reserved)

Figure 8: Lester in prison cells: Masturbating in the shower

Figure 9: Lester in prison cells: Watching Carolyn and Jim

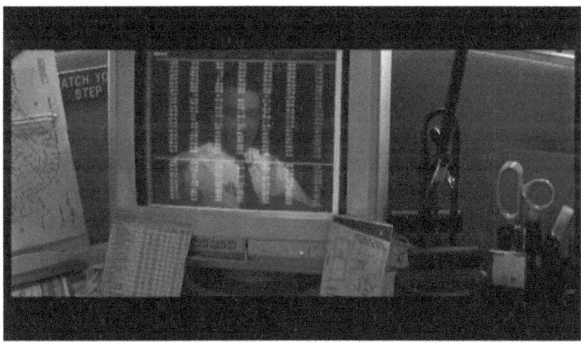

Figure 10: Lester in prison cells: At work.

Works Cited

Films:

Mendes, Sam; *American Beauty*. United States: Dreamworks SKG 1999.

Ross, Gary. *Pleasantville*. United States: New Line Cinema 1998.

Weir, Peter. *The Truman Show*. United States: Paramount Pictures 1998.

Bibliography:

Andrew, Dudley: *Concepts in Film Theory*. Oxford, New York: Oxford University Press 1984.

Armstrong, Richard. "'Where Am I Going to See Colours Like That?': Bliss, Desire and the Paintbox in *Pleasantville*". *Screen Education*, No. 52 (2008), pp. 155-160. Stable URL: http://search.informit.com.au/documentSummary;dn=724201414449829;res=IELHSS (Accessed April 4 2012).

Baccolini, Raffaella; Moylan, Tom. "Introduction. Dystopia and Histories". In: Baccolini, Raffaella; Moylan, Tom (Eds.). *Dark Horizons: Science Fiction and the Dystopian Imagination*. London: Routledge 2003, pp. 1-12.

Baudrillard, Jean. *America*. New York: Verso 1989.

Baudrillard, Jean. *Simulacra and Simulation*. Michigan: Michigan University Press 2010.

Baxandall, Rosalyn; Ewen, Elizabeth. *Picture Windows: How the Suburbs Happened*. New York: Basic Books 2000.

Benjamin, Rich. "The Gated Community Mentality". *New York Times Magazine*; March 30, 2012; New York Time, p. A27.

Berger, Bennet. *Looking for America: Essays on Youth, Suburbia and Other American Obsessions*. Englewood: Prentice Hall 1971.

Beuka, Robert. *SuburbiaNation: Reading Suburban Landscape in Twentieth-Century American Fiction and Film*. New York: Palgrave Macmillan 2004.

Beuka, Robert. "The View through the Picture Window: Surveillance and Entrapment Motifs in Suburban Film". In: Blauvelt, Andrew (Ed.). *Worlds Away. New Suburban Landscapes*. Minneapolis: Walker Art Center 2008, pp. 89-100.

Booker, Marvin Keith. *Dystopian Literature: A Theory and Research Guide*. Westport: Greenwood Press 1994.

Burgin, Victor. *In-different Spaces: Place and Memory in Visual Culture*. Berkeley: University of California Press 2000.

Brooks, David. "Our Sprawling, Supersize Utopia". *New York Times Magazine*; Apr 4, 2004; New York Time, p. 46.

Caldwell, Wilber. *Cynicism and the Evolution of the American Dream*. Washington: Potomac Books, Inc. 2006.

De Certeau, Michel. *The Practice of Everyday Life*. Berkeley: University of California Press 1984.

Deleuze, Gilles. *Negotiations*. Columbia University Press: New York 1990.

Deleuze, Gilles. "Postscript on the Societies of Control". *October*. Vol. 59. (Winter, 1992), pp. 3-7. Stable URL: http://www.jstor.org/stable/778828 (Accessed April 25, 2012).

Davis, Fred. *Yearning for Yesterday: A Sociology of Nostalgia*. New York: Free Press 1979.

Dickinson, Greg. "The Pleasantville Effect: Nostalgia and the Visual Framing of (White) Suburbia". *Western Journal of Communication*, 70, No. 3. (2006), pp. 212-233.

Ferns, Christopher. *Narrating Utopia: Ideology, Gender, Form in Utopian Literature*. Liverpool: Liverpool University Press 1999.

Fishman, Robert. *Bourgeois Utopias: The Rise and Fall of Suburbia*. New York: Basic Books 1987.

Fitting, Peter. "Unmasking the Real? Critique and Utopia in Recent SF Films". In: Baccolini, Raffaella; Moylan, Tom (Eds.). *Dark Horizons: Science Fiction and the Dystopian Imagination*. London: Routledge 2003, pp. 155-166.

Freese, Peter. *The American Dream and the American Nightmare*. Paderborn: Paderborner Universitätsreden 1987.

Foucault, Michel. "Panopticism". In: Rabinow, Paul (Ed.). *The Foucault Reader*. New York: Pantheon Books 1984, pp. 206-213.

Gallardo, Pere. "The Road to Perdition is Paved in Technicolour". In: Russell, Elizabeth (Ed.). *Trans/Forming Utopia: The 'Small Thin Story'*. Bern: Peter Lang 2009, pp 217-226.

Girling, Cynthia; Helphand, Kenneth. *Yard, Street, Park: The Design of Suburban Open Space*. New York: Wiley 1994.

Gordin, Michael; Tilley, Helen; Prakash, Gyan. "Utopia and Dystopia beyond Space and Time". In: Gordin, Michael; Tilley, Helen; Prakash, Gyan (Eds.). *Utopia/Dystopia. Conditions of Historical Possibility*. Princeton: Princeton University Press 2010.

Goudreau, Kim. "*American Beauty*: The Seduction of the Visual Image in the Culture of Technology". *Bulletin of Science, Technology & Society*. Vol. 26.1 (2006), pp. 23-30. Stable URL: http://www.sagepub.com/rpc2study/articles/Chapter04_Article07.pdf (Accessed April 25, 2012).

Gournelos, Ted. "Othering the Self: Dissonant Visual Culture and Quotidian Trauma in United States Suburbia". *Cultural Studies <=> Critical Methodologies*. Vol. 9, no. 4. August 2009, pp. 509-532. Stable URL: http://csc.sagepub.com/content/9/4/509.full.pdf (Accessed May 30, 2012).

Grosz, Elizabeth. *Space, Time and Perversion: Essays on the Politics of Bodies*. New York: Routledge 1995.

Halper, Thomas; Muzzio, Douglas. "Pleasantville? The Suburb and its Representation in American Movies". *Urban Affairs Review*, 37 (March 2002), pp. 543-574. Stable URL: uar.sagepub.com/content/37/4/543.full.pdf (Accessed April 15, 2012).

Harvard Law Review (Author unknown). "Locating the Suburb". *Harvard Law Review*, Vol. 117, No. 6 (Apr. 2004), pp. 2003-2022. Stable URL: http://www.jstor.org/stable/4093309 (Accessed April 28, 2012).

Hayden, Dolores. *Building Suburbia. Green Fields and Urban Growth, 1820-2000*. New York: Pantheon Books 2003.

Hayden, Dolores. *Redesigning the American Dream: The Future of Housing, Work, and Family Life*. New York: Norton 2002.

Hayward, Susan. *Cinema Studies: The Key Concepts*. New York: Routledge 2006.

Heath, Stephen. "Narrative Space". In: Rosen, Philip (Ed.). *Narrative, Apparatus, Ideology: A Film Theory Reader*. New York: Columbia University Press 1986, pp. 379-420.

Hewison, David. "Oh Rose, thou art sick! Anti-Individuation Forces in the Film *American Beauty*". *Journal of Analytical Psychology*, Vol. 48, No. 5. (Nov. 2003), pp. 683-704. Stable URL: http://onlinelibrary.wiley.com/doi/10.1111/1465-5922.00428/pdf (Accessed April 25, 2012)

Hutchinson, Sikivu. ""Look Closer": The White Spaces of American Beauty". *Spectator: The University of Southern California Journal of Film and Television Critics*, Vol.21.1. (Spring 2001), pp. 36-39.

Jackson, Kenneth. *Crabgrass Frontier: The Suburbanization of the United States*. New York: Oxford University Press 1985.

Jameson, Frederic. "Postmodernism and Consumer Society". In: Jameson, Frederic. *The Cultural Turn. Selected Writings on the Postmodern 1983-1998*. London: Verso 1998, pp.1-20.

Kammerer, Dietmar. *Bilder der Überwachung*. Frankfurt: Suhrkamp 2008.

Kennedy, David. "What the New Deal Did". *Political Science Quarterly*, Vol. 124, No. 2, 2009, pp.251-268.

Kenyon, Amy Maria. *Dreaming Suburbia: Detroit and the Production of Postwar Space and Culture*. Detroit: Wayne State University Press 2004.

Knox, Simone. "Reading *The Truman Show* Inside Out." *Film Criticism* 35, No. 1 (2010), pp. 1-23. Academic Search Premier, EBSCO host (Accessed March 21, 2012)

Kracauer, Siegfried. "The Establishment of Physical Existence". In: Braudy, Leo; Cohen, Marshall (Eds.). *Film Theory & Criticism*. Oxford: Oxford University Press 2009, pp. 262-272.

Kumar, Krishan. *Utopianism*. Minneapolis, MN: University of Minnesota Press 1991.

Law, Shirley. "Looking Closer: Structure, Style and Narrative in *American Beauty*". *Screen Education*, No. 43 (2006), pp.123-129. Stable URL: http://search.informit.com.au/documentSummary;dn=374186736020338;res=IELHSS (Accessed April 4 2012).

Lefebrve, Henri; Moore, Gerald (Trans.); Brenner, Neil (Ed.); Elden, Stuart (Ed.). *State, Space, World. Selected Essays*. Minneapolis: University of Minnesota Press 2009.

Lefebrve, Henri. Nicholson-Smith, Donald (Trans.). *The Production of Space*. Oxford: Blackwell 1991.

Levitas, Ruth. "The Archive of the Feet: Memory, Place and Utopia". In: Griffin, Michael; Moylan, Tom (Eds.). *Exploring the Utopian Impulse: Essays on Utopian Thought and Practice*. Peter Lang: Bern 2007; pp. 19-42.

Low, Setha. *Behind the Gates: Life, Security, and the Pursuit of Happiness in Fortress America*. New York, NY: Routledge 2003.

Martinson, Tom. *American Dreamscape: The Pursuit of Happiness in Postwar Suburbia*. New York, NY: Carroll & Graf Publishers 2000.

Marks, Peter. "Imagining Surveillance: Utopian Visions and Surveillance Studies". *Surveillance & Society*, 3 (2005), pp. 222-239. Stable URL: http://www.surveillance-and-society.org/Articles3%282%29/imagining.pdf (Accessed April 30, 2012),

Mercadante, Linda. "The God behind the Screen: *Pleasantville* & *The Truman Show*". *Journal of Religion and Film*, Vol. 5, No. 2 (October 2001). Stable URL: http://www.unomaha.edu/jrf/truman.htm (Accessed April 4, 2012).

Müller, André. *Film und Utopie: Positionen des Fiktionalen Films zwischen Gattungstraditionen und Gesellschaftlichen Zukunftsdiskursen*. Münster: LIT Verlag 2010.

O'Gorman, Marcel. "*American Beauty* Busted: Necromedia and Domestic Discipline". *SubStance*, Vol. 33, No. 3, Issue 105: Special Issue: Overload (2004), pp. 34-51. Stable URL: http://www.jstor.org/stable/3685544 (Accessed April 15, 2012).

Porter, Robert. "Habermas in *Pleasantville*: Cinema as Political Critique". *Contemporary Political Theory*, 13.2 (2007), pp. 405-418. Stable URL: http://www.palgrave-journals.com/cpt/journal/v6/n4/pdf/9300300a.pdf (Accessed April 15, 2012).

Reinhartz, Adele. *Scripture on the Silver Screen*. Louisville: Westminster John Know Press 2003.

Sargent, Lyman. "The three faces of Utopianism Revisited". *Utopian Studies*, Vol. 5, No. 1 (1994), pp. 1-37. Stable URL: http://www.jstor.org/stable/20719246 (Accessed April 20, 2012)

Smith, David. "'Beautiful Necessities': *American Beauty* and the Idea of Freedom". *Journal of Religion and Film*, Vol. 6, No. 2 (October 2002). Stable URL: http://www.unomaha.edu/jrf/am.beauty.htm (Accessed April 4, 2012).

Smith, Michael. *Reading Simulacra: Fatal Theories for Postmodernity*. Albany: State University of New York Press 2001.

Spector, Judith; Tsiopos Willis, Katherine. "The Aesthetics of Materialism in Alan Ball's *American Beauty*." *Midwest Quarterly*. 48, no. 2 (2007), pp. 279-96.

Spigel, Lynn. *Welcome to the Dreamhouse: Popular Media and Postwar Suburbs*. Durham: Duke University Press 2001.

Spigel, Lynn. "From Theatre to Space Ship. Metaphors of Suburban Domesticity in Postwar America". In: Silverstone, Roger. (Ed.). *Visions of Suburbia*. London and New York: Routledge 1997.

Wise, J. Macgregor. "Mapping the Culture of Control. Seeing through *The Truman Show*". *Television and New Media* 2002; Vol. 3, No. 1, pp. 29-47. Stable URL: http://www.sagepub.com/mcdonaldizationstudy5/articles/McDonaldization_Articles%20PDFs/Wise.pdf (Accessed on April 14, 2012)

Websites:

"Westec - Digital Surveillance Systems" (Accessed April 15, 2012)
    <http://www.westec.net/>

"Pleasantville Script by Gary Ross" (Accessed April 15, 2012)
    <http://www.imsdb.com/scripts/Pleasantville.html>

"The Truman Show" (Accessed April 15, 2012)
    <http://www.virtualworldlets.net/Resources/Hosted/Resource.php?Name=TheTrumanSh
    ow>

"American Beauty Rose" (Accessed April 15, 2012)
    <http://backyardgardener.com/plantname/pda_fb10.html>

"American Beauty Script by Allan Ball" (Accessed April 15, 2012)
    <http://www.dailyscript.com/scripts/AmericanBeauty_final.html>